National Contract Management Association

Desktop Guide to Basic Contracting Terms

Third Edition, Revised and Expanded

Compiled by Regina Mickells Bova, CPCM

Edited by Anne M. Rankin

Reviewed by: David L. Balint, CPCM
Teledyne Brown Engineering

©1989; 1990; 1992 National Contract Management Association. All rights reserved
1912 Woodford Road, Vienna, VA 22182. 703/448-9231 or 800/344-8096
Printed in the United States of America
ISBN 0-940343-30-4

INTRODUCTION

Although the 1992 edition of NCMA's *Desktop Guide to Basic Contracting Terms* provides useful information on the fundamental meaning and everyday use of more than 800 procurement terms, the *Guide* is *not* meant to provide complete technical definitions, especially as they apply to various specialized contracting situations. Readers are encouraged to refer to the *Federal Acquisition Regulation* and other official sources for more detailed definitions.

This *Desktop Guide to Basic Contracting Terms* can serve as an on-the-job reference for new entrants into the field, a review for more seasoned practitioners, and a study tool for the Certified Associate Contracts Manager (CACM) Examination. In addition, those preparing for the Certified Professional Contracts Manager (CPCM) Examination may refer to this *Guide* as a starting point when they answer the practice exam questions available in NCMA's *CPCM Candidate's Workbook* and its *Supplements*.

The contract management profession relies largely on precision and proper interpretation of language. Therefore, this edition of *Desktop Guide to Basic Contracting Terms* has been expanded to cover definitions from the broad range of disciplines a contract manager may expect to encounter—from contract administration to quality to finance to law.

We invite readers to submit additional terms for inclusion in future editions of this publication. If you are able to provide an existing written definition along with the term itself, please provide a reference for the definition.

INDEX TO SOURCE CODES

AFIT	Air Force Institute of Technology. *Compendium of Authenticated Systems and Logistics Terms, Definitions and Acronyms.* Wright-Patterson Air Force Base, OH: Air Force Institute of Technology, 1981.
AH	*American Heritage Dictionary.* 2d college ed. Boston: Houghton Mifflin Company, 1982.
ASPM	Department of Defense. *Armed Services Pricing Manual.* "Vol. 1, Contract Pricing." Washington, DC: Department of Defense, 1986.
BLD	Black, Henry C. *Black's Law Dictionary.* 5th ed. St. Paul, MN: West Publishing Co., 1979.
BLD2	Black, Henry C. *Black's Law Dictionary.* 6th ed. St. Paul, MN: West Publishing Co., 1990.
BOE	*Business Conduct Guidelines.* Seattle, WA: The Boeing Company, 1987.
BOE II	*Desktop Guide for Continuous Quality Improvement.* Seattle, WA: Boeing Defense and Space Group, 1990.
BP(89-13)	Vacketta, Carl L., Richard H. Mays, and Gail D. Frulla. "The Government Contractor Defense in Environmental Actions." *Briefing Papers* (no. 89-13). Washington, DC: Federal Publications, Inc., December 1989.
BP(90-11)	Albertson, Terry L., Edward Jackson, and Linda S. Bruggeman. "Compensation Costs." *Briefing Papers* (no. 90-11). Washington, DC: Federal Publications, Inc., October 1990.
BP(91-8)	Allen, Rand L., and Jeffrey M. Villet. "Implied Warranty of Specifications." *Briefing Papers* (no. 91-8). Washington, DC: Federal Publications, Inc., July 1991.
CE	Stewart, Rodney D. *Cost Estimating.* 2d ed. New York: John Wiley & Sons, Inc., 1991.
Cohen	Cohen, Cary. *The Handbook of Effective Contract Administration.* Richmond, VA: Caldwell Consulting Associates, 1985.
Culver	Culver, C. M. *Federal Government Procurement—An Unchartered Course Through Turbulent Waters.* McLean, VA: National Contract Management Association, 1985.
DBL	Dobler, Donald W., David N. Burt, and Lamar Lee, Jr. *Purchasing and Materials Management.* 5th ed. New York: McGraw-Hill Publications, 1990.
DLA	Defense Logistics Agency. "Understanding the DOD Budget." *Dimensions.* Alexandria, VA: Defense Logistics Agency (April 1991): 2-3.

DOD	Office of the Inspector General. *Acquisition Alerts for Program Managers.* Washington, DC: Department of Defense, 1987.
DOD-MMH	Defense Systems Management College. *Department of Defense Manufacturing Management Handbook for Program Managers.* 2d ed. Fort Belvoir, VA: Defense Systems Management College, 1984.
DSMC	Defense Systems Management College. *Subcontracting Management Handbook.* Ft. Belvoir, VA: Department of Defense, 1988.
ECON	Waud, Roger N. *Microeconomics.* 3d ed. New York: Harper & Row, Publishers, 1986.
EDI	Emmelhainz, Margaret A. *Electronic Data Interchange: A Total Management Guide.* New York: Van Nostrand Reinhold, 1990.
EDIW	*EDI World.* Hollywood, FL: EDI World, Inc. • (1-11)—Ugljesa, Joan M. "A&D Contract Management Discovers EDI." Vol. 1, no. 11 (November 1991): 25. • (2-1)—Millhorn, Tom, and Javier Romeu. "EDI Capabilities Grow to Include Complex Data Transfer." Vol. 2, no. 1 (January 1992): 31.
FAI	Federal Acquisition Institute. *Basic Procurement Course Materials.* Washington, DC: Federal Acquisition Institute, 1991.
FAI II	Federal Acquisition Institute. *Small Purchase Procurement: An Introduction.* "Desk Guide and Workbook." Washington, DC: Federal Acquisition Institute, 1986.
FAR	*Federal Acquisition Regulation.*
FBL	Scaletta, Phillip J., Jr., and George D. Cameron III. *Foundations of Business Law.* 2d ed. Homewood, IL: Richard D. Irwin, Inc., 1990.
FIRMR	*Federal Information Resources Management Regulations,* 41 C.F.R., Chapter 201.
Foglia	Foglia, Joseph T. *How to Market to the Government.* Richmond, VA: Baruch Defense Marketing, Inc., 1989.
GAO	U.S. General Accounting Office. *Quality Assurance Concerns About Four Navy Missile Systems.* Washington, DC: United States General Accounting Office, 1987.
GSA	U.S. General Services Administration. *Small Purchases/Schedule Contracts Student Manual (#220A).* Washington, DC: U.S. General Services Administration, January 1989.
GUIDE	Arnavas, Donald P., and William J. Ruberry. *Government Contract Guidebook.* Washington, DC: Federal Publications, Inc., 1986.
JIG	*Cost/Schedule Control Systems Criteria Joint Implementation Guide.* Washington, DC: Departments of the Air Force, Army, Navy, Defense Logistics Agency, and Defense Contract Audit Agency, October 1987.
L&P	Lamm, David V., and William C. Pursch. "A Dictionary of Contracting Terms." *Contract Management* (May 1991): 41.

L&P II	Lamm, David V., and William C. Pursch. "A Dictionary of Contracting Terms Part II." *Contract Management* (November 1991): 42.
McVay	McVay, Barry L. *Getting Started in Federal Contracting.* Westbury, NY: Asher-Gallant Press, 1986.
MGMT	Horngren, Charles T., and Gary L. Sundem. *Introduction to Management Accounting.* 7th ed. Englewood Cliffs, NJ: Prentice-Hall, 1987.
MSA	Boyd, Stuart R., and Juan A. Montes. *The Management of Security Assistance.* 8th ed. Wright-Patterson AFB, OH: Defense Institute of Security Assistance Management, February 1988.
Navy	Richardson, Judith V. *Handbook for Contract Specialists.* Washington, DC: Naval Air Systems Command, 1989.
NC-A	Cibinic, John, Jr., and Ralph C. Nash, Jr. *Administration of Government Contracts.* Washington, DC: George Washington University, 1985.
NC-F	Cibinic, John, Jr., and Ralph C. Nash, Jr. *Formation of Government Contracts.* Washington, DC: George Washington University, 1982.
NCMA-CA	*Cost Accounting Basics.* Partially revised. Vienna, Va: National Contract Management Association, 1990.
NCMA-CP2	*CPCM Candidate's Workbook Supplement 2.* Vienna, VA: National Contract Management Association, 1989.
NCMA-PSP	*Practical Small Purchasing.* Vienna, VA: National Contract Management Association, 1991.
NCMA-SB	*Solicitations, Bids & Awards.* McLean, VA: National Contract Management Association, 1984.
NCMA-SC	*Subcontracts: Government and Industry Issues.* Vienna, VA: National Contract Management Association, 1989.
NCMA-SP	*Specifications and Standards.* McLean, VA: National Contract Management Association, 1984.
NCMA-SS	*Source Selection.* McLean, VA: National Contract Management Association, 1984.
NES92	Hernandez, Richard J., and Delane F. Moeller. *Negotiating a Quality Contract.* Vienna, VA: National Contract Management Association, 1991.
OMB	Office of Management and Budget. *OMB Circular No. A-109.* "Major Systems Acquisitions." Washington, DC: Office of Management and Budget, April 5, 1976.
OPM	U.S. Office of Personnel Management. *Position Classification Standards for the Contract and Procurement Series, GS-1102.* Washington, DC: U.S. Office of Personnel Management, 1981.
PW	Price Waterhouse. *Contracting with the Federal Government.* 2d ed. New York: John Wiley & Sons, 1988.

Sherman	Sherman, Stanley N. *Contract Management: Post Award*. Gaithersburg, MD: Wordcrafters Publications, 1987.
Sherman2	Sherman, Stanley N. *Government Procurement Management*. 2d ed. Gaithersburg, MD: Wordcrafters Publications, 1985.
Sherman3	Sherman, Stanley N. *Government Procurement Management*. Gaithersburg, MD: Wordcrafters Publications, 1991.
Steinhauer	Steinhauer, Raleigh Fred. "The Intergovernmental Cooperative Purchasing Arrangement in the Metropolitan Washington Area." *A Dissertation Submitted to the School of Government and Business Administration*. Washington, DC: The George Washington University, May 1972.
TIPS	*Topical Issues in Procurement Series*. Vienna, VA: National Contract Management Association. • (1-6)—"Controlling Consultants." Vol. 1, no. 6 (March 1990). • (1-9)—"Environmental Issues in Government Contracting." Vol. 1, no. 9 (June 1990). • (1-12)—"Who's Reading Your Mail? A Freedom of Information Act Update." Vol. 1, no. 12 (September 1990). • (1-14)—"Technology Transfer and Cooperative Research and Development Agreements." Vol. 1, no. 14 (November 1990). • (1-15)—"The Trade Agreements Act." Vol. 1, no. 15 (December 1990). • (2-5)—"The Data Rights Rollercoaster." Vol. 2, no. 5 (May 1991). • (2-6)—"The Mystery of the M Account." Vol. 2, no. 6 (June 1991). • (2-8)—"Expert Systems Applications in the Procurement Field." Vol. 2, no. 8 (August 1991). • (2-9)—"The Pilot Mentor-Protege Program." Vol. 2, no. 9 (September 1991). • (2-10)—"Exploring Export Opportunities." Vol. 2, no. 10 (October 1991). • (2-11)—"Uncompensated Overtime: Who Pays the Price?" Vol. 2, no. 11 (November 1991). • (2-12)—"Contending with Contract Changes." Vol. 2, no. 12 (December 1991). • (3-2)—"Preserving the Industrial Base." Vol. 3, no. 2 (February 1992). • (3-3)—"ADPE Contracting: An Acquisition Anomaly." Vol. 3, no. 3 (March 1992). • (3-4)—"Bid Protests at the GAO and the GSBCA." Vol. 3, no. 4 (April 1992). • (3-5)—"Best Value Contracting." Vol. 3, no. 5 (May 1992).
UNI	Unisys Defense Systems. *Handbook of Ethical Business Practices*. McLean, VA: Unisys Corporation, 1988.

COMMON ACRONYMS

A-76—Office of Management and Budget (OMB) Circular Number A-76, Performance of Commercial Activities

A-109—Office of Management and Budget (OMB) Circular Number A-109, Major Systems Acquisition

A-120—Office of Management and Budget (OMB) Circular Number A-120, Guidelines for the Use of Advisory and Assistance Services

AAC—Advance Acquisition Contract

ACO—Administrative Contracting Officer

ADP—Automatic Data Processing

ADPE—Automatic Data Processing Equipment

AFARS—Army FAR Supplement

AFFARS—Air Force FAR Supplement

APR—Agency Procurement Request

ASPR—Armed Services Procurement Regulation

BAFO—Best and Final Offer

BCWP—Budgeted Cost for Work Performed

BCWS—Budgeted Cost for Work Scheduled

BOA—Basic Ordering Agreement

BOM—Bill of Materials

CAAC—Civilian Agency Acquisition Council

CAD/CAM—Computer-Aided Design/Computer-Aided Manufacturing

CAGE Code— Commercial and Government Entity Code

CALS—Computer-Aided Acquisition and Logistics Support

CAO—Contract Administration Office

CAR—Commerce Acquisition Regulation

CASB—Cost Accounting Standards Board

CCP—Contract Change Proposal

CDR—Critical Design Review

CDRL—Contract Data Requirements List

CFR—Code of Federal Regulations

CICA—Competition in Contracting Act

CO—Contracting Officer

COC—Certificate of Competency

COCO—Contractor Owned, Contractor Operated

COGP—Commission on Government Procurement

COTR—Contracting Officer's Technical Representative

COTS—Commercial-off-the-Shelf

CPAF—Cost-Plus-Award-Fee

CPBOSH—Committee for the Purchase from the Blind and Other Severely Handicapped

CPFF—Cost-Plus-Fixed-Fee

CPIF—Cost-Plus-Incentive-Fee

CPM—Critical Path Method

CPPC—Cost-Plus-Percentage-of-Cost

CPSR—Contractor Purchasing System Review

CRAG—Contractor Risk Assessment Guide
C/SCSC—Cost/Schedule Control Systems Criteria
DAC—Defense Acquisition Circular
DAR—Defense Acquisition Regulation
DARC—Defense Acquisition Regulatory Council
DD FORM—Department of Defense Form
DEAR—Department of Energy Acquisition Regulation
DFARS—Department of Defense FAR Supplement
DLA—Defense Logistics Agency
DLAR—Defense Logistics Acquisition Regulation
DOD—Department of Defense
DPA—Delegation of Procurement Authority
DPAS—Defense Priorities and Allocations System
EAC—Estimate at Completion
EAJA—Equal Access to Justice Act
EAR—Export Administration Regulation
ECP—Engineering Change Proposal
EDI—Electronic Data Interchange
EFT—Electronic Funds Transfer
E-Mail—Electronic Mail
EOQ—Economic Order Quantity
EPAAR—Environmental Protection Agency Acquisition Regulation
FAC—Federal Acquisition Circular
FAD Sheet—Financial Data Addendum Sheet
FAI—Federal Acquisition Institute
FAR—Federal Acquisition Regulation
FASB—Financial Accounting Standards Board
FCCM—Facilities Capital Cost of Money
FDPC—Federal Data Processing Center
FFP—Firm-Fixed-Price
FIFO—First In, First Out
FIRMR—Federal Information Resources Management Regulation
FMS—Foreign Military Sales
FOB—Free on Board
FOIA—Freedom of Information Act
FPDC—Federal Procurement Data Center
FPI—Fixed-Price-Incentive
FPR—Fixed-Price Redeterminable; *also* Federal Procurement Regulations
FSD—Full-Scale Development
G&A—General and Administrative
GAAP—Generally Accepted Accounting Principles
GAO—General Accounting Office
GFE—Government-Furnished Equipment
GFP—Government-Furnished Property
GOCO—Government-Owned, Contractor-Operated
GPLR—Government Purpose License Rights
GSA—General Services Administration
GSAR—General Services Administration Acquisition Regulation

HUDAR—Department of Housing and Urban Development Acquisition Regulation

IDIQ—Indefinite Delivery/ Indefinite Quantity

IFB—Invitation for Bids

ILS—Integrated Logistics Support

IMIP—Industrial Modernization Incentives Program

IOT—Interorganizational Transfer

IR&D—Independent Research and Development

ITAR—International Traffic in Arms Regulation

J&A—Justification and Approval

JAR—Justice Acquisition Regulation

JIT—Just in Time

JWOD—Javits-Wagner-O'Day Act

LIFO—Last In, First Out

LOE—Level of Effort

LOI—Letter of Intent

MANTECH—Manufacturing Technology

MILSPEC—Military Specification

MILSTRIP—Military Standard Requisitioning and Issue Procedures

MMAS—Material Management and Accounting System

MOA—Memorandum of Agreement

MOU—Memorandum of Understanding

MRP—Material Requirements Planning

NAPS—Navy Acquisition Procedures Supplement

NASA FAR Supplement—National Aeronautics and Space Administration FAR Supplement

NDI—Non-Developmental Item

NTE—Not to Exceed

OCI—Organizational Conflict of Interest

OFPP—Office of Federal Procurement Policy

PALT—Procurement Administrative Lead Time

PCA- Physical Configuration Audit

PCO—Procuring Contracting Officer

PERT—Program Evaluation and Review Technique

PL—Public Law

PM—Program Manager

PMB—Performance Measurement Baseline

PNM—Price Negotiation Memorandum

PO—Purchase Order

PR—Purchase Request; Purchase Requisition

PRR—Production Readiness Review

QBL—Qualified Bidders List

QML—Qualified Manufacturers List

QPL—Qualified Products List

R&D—Research and Development

RDT&E—Research, Development, Test, & Evaluation

REA—Request for Equitable Adjustment

RFP—Request for Proposal

RFQ—Request for Quotation

ROI—Return on Investment

SADBUS—Small and Disadvantaged Business Utilization Specialist

SBA—Small Business Act; *also* Small Business Administration

SBIR—Small Business Innovation Research Program

SCDRL or SDRL—Subcontractor's Data Requirements List

SDB—Small Disadvantaged Business

SF—Standard Form

SOW—Statement of Work

SPC—Statistical Process Control

SSA—Source Selection Authority

SSAC—Source Selection Advisory Council

SSEB—Source Selection Evaluation Board

SSP—Source Selection Plan

TAPR—Treasury Acquisition Procurement Regulation

TAR—Department of Transportation Acquisition Regulation

TCO—Termination Contracting Officer

TINA—Truth in Negotiations Act

TQM—Total Quality Management

VAAR—Veterans Affairs Acquisition Regulation

VE—Value Engineering

VECP—Value Engineering Change Proposal

WBS—Work Breakdown Structure

WGM—Weighted Guidelines Method

ZBB—Zero-Based Budgeting

— A —

ABSORPTION OF COSTING A method of determining the actual cost of a unit of production (either at various stages of completion or when service is provided), which treats fixed indirect costs as product costs. Under absorption costing, a unit's total cost is equal to the sum of the allocated fixed indirect costs and the costs of direct material, direct labor, and applicable overhead. [L&P II]

ABSTRACT OF BIDS A list of the bidders for a particular sealed bid procurement showing the significant portions of their bids. [GUIDE]

ACCELERATED DELIVERY The advancing, in whole or in part, of the scheduled delivery of material on order to meet emergency requirements. [AFIT]

ACCELERATED PROCEDURE Procedure under the Contract Disputes Act whereby an appellant before an agency Board of Contract Appeals can elect, for certain claims, to have a decision issued on a claim within six months after making the election. [GUIDE]

Also known as "Expedited Procedure."

ACCEPTANCE (1) The act of an authorized government [buyer] representative by which the government [buyer] assents to ownership of existing and identified supplies, or approves specific services rendered, as partial or complete performance of a contract. [AFIT]

(2) An offeree's manifestation of assent to the terms of an offer made to him or her by an offeror. The acceptance is the act, the oral or written assent, or, in certain instances, the silence that creates contractual liabilities for both the offeror and the offeree. [FBL]

ACCEPTANCE, IMPLIED In the case of a bilateral contract, acceptance of an offer need not be expressed, but may be shown by any words or acts indicating the offeree's assent to the proposed bargain. [BLD]

ACCEPTANCE SAMPLING Evaluating a portion of a lot for the purpose of accepting or rejecting the entire lot as either conforming or not conforming to a quality specification. [BOE II]

ACCORD AND SATISFACTION (1) A method of discharging a claim whereby the parties agree to give and accept something in settlement of the claim and perform the agreement. The accord is the agreement and the satisfaction is the execution or performance. [BLD]

(2) Two persons agree that one of them has a right of action against the other, but they accept a substitute or different act or value as performance. [FBL]

ACCOUNTING ENTITY The accounting process recognizes various enterprises (i.e., companies, government units, etc.) as individual entities, and that economic activity relating to these entities can be separately identified and measured distinctly from other entities. The accounting entity concept does not apply only to the identification and segregation of economic activity among different enterprises; it may refer to distinctions between departments within a company, individuals within a department, segments within a conglomeration, etc. [NCMA-CA]

ACCOUNTING PERIOD The accounting process recognizes the necessity of providing financial information over specified time periods. This facilitates a comparison of the entity's performance between time periods and provides relevant financial information on a timely basis to be used in managerial decisions. [NCMA-CA]

ACCOUNTING PRINCIPLES BOARD (APB) See "Financial Accounting Standards Board."

ACCOUNTING SYSTEM A formal communications network that supplies relevant information for planning, control, decision-making, and evaluation. [NCMA-CA]

ACCRUAL ACCOUNTING The accrual basis of accounting recognizes important concepts, such as receivables due from customers, payables due to vendors, interest due from investments, and other "matching" concepts as a means of providing an accurate picture of a company's financial (economic) position. [NCMA-CA]

See also "Matching Principle."

ACQUISITION (1) A process that begins with establishment of needs and includes the description of requirements, solicitations and source selection, contract award, contract financing, contract performance, contract administration, and all technical and management functions directly related to the process of fulfilling an organization's needs by contract. [AFIT]
(2) The process of obtaining supplies, services, or systems by contract with appropriated funds, whether the supplies, services, or systems exist or must be created. [NCMA-SS]
ACQUISITION GOALS See "Goals of the Acquisition Process."
ACQUISITION PLAN A plan for an acquisition that serves as the basis for initiating the individual contracting actions necessary to acquire a system or support a program. [FAI]
ACQUISITION PLANNING The process by which efforts of all personnel responsible for an acquisition are coordinated and integrated through a comprehensive plan for fulfilling the agency need in a timely manner at a reasonable cost. It includes developing the overall strategy for managing the acquisition. [FAR]
ACQUISITION PROGRAM A directed effort funded either through procurement appropriation, or a research, development, test, and evaluation appropriation with the goal of providing a new or improved capability for a validated need. An acquisition program may include either development or procurement or modifications of systems, subsystems, equipment, or components, as well as supporting equipment, systems, projects, and studies. [DSMC]
ACQUISITION RISK The chance that some element of an acquisition program produces an unintended result with an adverse effect on system effectiveness, suitability cost, or availability for deployment. [DSMC]
ACQUISITION STRATEGY The conceptual framework for conducting systems acquisition. It encompasses the broad concepts and objectives that direct and control the overall development, production, and deployment of a system. Required by OMB Circular A-109 and government department directives for virtually all programs. [DSMC]
ACQUISITION STREAMLINING Any action that results in more efficient and effective use of resources to develop, produce, and deploy quality systems and products. This includes ensuring that only cost effective requirements are included, at the most appropriate time, in system and equipment solicitations and contracts. [DSMC]
ACTION PLAN The steps a team develops to implement a solution or the actions needed to make continued progress toward a solution. [BOE II]
ACTIVE CONTRACT Any contract that has been awarded and on which any element of contractor performance, payment, or administrative closing action is outstanding. [AFIT]
ACTIVITY ACCOUNTING See "Responsibility Accounting."
ACTUAL AUTHORITY See "Agent Authority."
ADJUSTED CEILING A negotiated adjustment to the ceiling price for changes that reflect a change in the negotiated maximum liability of the government. [AFIT]
See also "Negotiated Ceiling."
ADJUSTED TARGET Accumulated price resulting from changes to the basic contract for in-program change, change in scope, and/or terminations reflecting the current negotiated target price for work authorized. [AFIT]
ADMINISTRATING CONTRACTING OFFICER (ACO) The government contracting officer, often at an installation other than the one making the contract, who is authorized to perform postaward contract administration duties, monitor contractor's performance, and perform postaward contractual functions delegated by the purchasing office. [DSMC, OPM]
ADMINISTRATIVE CHANGE A unilateral contract change, in writing, that does not affect the substantive rights of the parties, such as a change in the paying office or the appropriation data. [FAR]
ADMINISTRATIVE COSTS General overhead expenses incident to the issue, sale, and transfer of material. [AFIT]
ADMINISTRATIVE LEAD TIME The time interval between initiation of pro-

curement action and letting [award] of contract or placing of order. [AFIT]
See also "Procurement Lead Time."

ADVANCE ACQUISITION CONTRACT (AAC) A preliminary contract committing the contractor to proceed with an effort, including planning and engineering, placement of orders for material, and other production effort necessary to protect the required delivery schedule for the contract end items cited in the contract. Used when the lead time is too long to allow waiting for funds in the fiscal year for which the end items are to be procured. Long lead funds are specifically appropriated for this type of effort. The definitive contract is negotiated at a later date and supersedes the AAC. [Navy]

ADVANCE AGREEMENT An agreement between the contractor and the government regarding the treatment of specified costs negotiated either before or during contract performance but preferably before the cost covered by the agreement is incurred. [PW]

ADVANCE BUY Procurement to provide for components that require a longer lead time than the system of which they are a part. [AFIT]

ADVANCE PAYMENT An advance of money made by the government to a contractor prior to, in anticipation of, and for the purpose of performance under a contract. [OPM]

ADVANCE PAYMENT BOND This bond secures fulfillment of the contractor's obligations under an advance payment provision. [FAR]

ADVANCE PROCUREMENT PLAN A plan of procurement accomplishment showing the method of procurement, the general time table, and the expected price. [OPM]

ADVANCED DEVELOPMENT Projects that have advanced to a point where the development of experimental hardware for technical or operational testing is required prior to the determination of whether these items should be designed or engineered for eventual use. [AFIT]

AFFILIATES Associated business concerns or individuals if, directly or indirectly, (a) either one controls or can control the other, or (b) a third party controls or can control both. [FAR]

AFFIRMATIVE ACTION PLAN A plan submitted with a bid, under which the bidder agrees to use its best efforts to employ certain percentages of minority workers. [GUIDE]

AGENCY A relationship whereby the principal authorizes another (the agent) to act for and on behalf of the principal and to bind the principal in contract. [FBL]
See also "Agent Authority."

AGENCY PROCUREMENT REQUEST (APR) A request by a federal agency for the General Services Administration (GSA) to acquire Automatic Data Processing Equipment (ADPE), commercially available software, maintenance services, and commercial ADP services, or for GSA to delegate the authority to acquire these items. [FIRMR]

AGENT AUTHORITY The power delegated by a principal to his or her agent; a right to exercise power. *Actual authority*: Authority that the principal intentionally confers on the agent or allows the agent to believe him- or herself to possess. *Apparent authority*: The principal knowingly permits the agent to exercise authority, though not actually granted. *Express authority*: Authority delegated to an agent intentionally, distinctly, plainly; expressed orally, or in writing. *Implied authority*: Authority implied from the principal's conduct; it includes only such acts as are incident and necessary to the exercise of the authority expressly granted. [BLD]
See also "Agency."

AGING SCHEDULE A report of the status of invoices that are outstanding. Used in collection activities. [Cohen]

ALLOCABLE COST A cost whose relative benefits make it assignable or chargeable to one or more of the cost objectives agreed to between contractual parties. [OPM]

ALLOCATE Assignment of an item of cost, or a group of cost items, to one or more cost objectives for both direct and indirect costs. [FAR]

ALLOWABLE COSTS A cost that is reasonable, allocable, within accepted standards, or otherwise conforms to generally accepted accounting principles, specific limitations or exclusions, or agreed-to terms between contractual parties. [OPM]

ALTERNATE BID One of two or more bids on the same item, submitted on different bases by the same bidder, as provided by the invitation to bid. [AFIT]

ALTERNATE ITEM An item selected by the responsible engineering activity in lieu of the forecast item. [AFIT]

AMENDMENT A change (correction, deletion, or addition) to any information contained in an IFB or RFP (or previous amendment thereto). The amendment becomes part of the solicitation and any resulting contract. [FAI] See also "Contract Modification."

AMORTIZATION The gradual reduction, redemption, or liquidation of the balance of an account according to a specified schedule of time and amounts. [AFIT]

ANTICIPATED REIMBURSEMENT The amount of reimbursements expected to be earned and added to appropriation or other funding authority as a source of funds in order to cover obligations incurred in performance of work, services, procurement of material for others, or material delivered from stock. [AFIT]

ANTICIPATORY PROFIT Profits payable for work not performed. This payment is viewed as a reasonable sanction to be imposed upon defaulters in ordinary contractual relationships. The Termination for Convenience clause established for government contracts bars payment of anticipatory profit. [Sherman]

ANTICIPATORY REPUDIATION When the contractor [supplier], without justification, makes a positive statement to the government [buyer] that it will not perform its contractual duties. [BLD]

ANTI-DEFICIENCY ACT A regulation prohibiting the obligation of government money in advance of an appropriation or in excess of the amount of an available appropriation. [DOD]

ANTI-KICKBACK ACT Legislation designed to deter subcontractors from making payments to influence the award of subcontracts, 41 U.S.C. 51-54. [FAR]
  Also known as "Copeland Anti-Kickback Act."

ANTITRUST ACTS Federal and state statutes to protect trade and commerce from unlawful restraints, price discriminations, price fixing, and monopolies. Most states have mini-antitrust acts patterned on the federal acts. The principal federal antitrust acts are the Sherman Act (1890); the Clayton Act (1914); the Federal Trade Commission Act (1914); and the Robinson-Patman Act (1936). [BLD]

ANTITRUST VIOLATIONS Anticompetitive practices such as collusive bidding, follow-the-leader pricing, rotated low bids, and collusive price estimating systems, are antitrust violations. [FAR]

APPARENT AUTHORITY See "Agent Authority."

APPEAL Resort to a superior (i.e., appellate court) to review the decision of an inferior (i.e., trial) court or administrative agency. [BLD]

APPEAL NOTICE A notice to a Board of Contract Appeals that a contracting officer's final decision will be appealed. [GUIDE]

APPORTIONMENT The Office of Management and Budget (OMB) distributes funds to federal agencies for obligation. An agency may not obligate more funds than it receives. [DLA]

APPROPRIATION BILL (1) Passed by Congress and signed by the president, this bill tells an agency how much it can spend on a program. This law actually gives the agency the funds to pay the bills. [DLA]
  (2) After an appropriation is enacted by Congress, the Office of Management and Budget (OMB) divides those appropriated funds on a quarterly basis to the various executive organizations through a process called apportionment. Departments and agencies then allocate funds throughout their respective organizations. [TIPS(2-6)]

ARBITRATION (1) A nonjudicial method for settling matters of disputes between parties. [Cohen]
  (2) Procedure whereby a dispute is referred to one or more impartial persons (selected by the disputing parties) for a final and binding determination. [GUIDE]
  (3) To settle a dispute, an appointed arbitrator (third person) comes in to help the parties make an out-of-court decision. This saves the time and expense of litigation. [FBL]

ARBITRATOR A third person chosen to decide a dispute between two other persons. [FBL]

ARMED SERVICES PROCUREMENT ACT General federal statute enacted in 1947 that governs contracting by the Department of Defense and its military services. [GUIDE]

ARMED SERVICES PROCUREMENT REGULATION (ASPR) Set of procurement regulations issued in 1949 that once governed procurements by military agencies and that later (in 1978) became known as the Defense Acquisition Regulation (DAR). [GUIDE]

ASSEMBLAGE A collection of items that is designed to accomplish one general function and is identified and issued as a single item. [AFIT]

ASSETS Property of all kinds (real and personal, tangible and intangible), including, among other things, for certain purposes, patents and causes of action that belong to any person, including a corporation and the estate of a decedent. The entire property of a person, association, corporation, or estate that is applicable or subject to the payment of his or her debts. [BLD]

ASSIGNMENT A transfer of rights (usually contract rights) from an assignor to an assignee. [FBL]

ASSIST AUDIT An audit performed by one audit office at the request of another audit office; usually an adjunct to or an integral part of an audit being performed by the requestor. [OPM]

ATTRITION The loss of a resource due to natural causes in the normal course of events, such as a turnover of employees or spoilage and obsolescence of material. [DOD-MMH]

AUCTION TECHNIQUES Federal government personnel shall not engage in auction techniques such as (a) indicating to an offeror a cost or price that it must meet to obtain further consideration; (b) advising an offeror of its price standing relative to another offeror (however, it is permissible to inform an offeror that its cost or price is considered by the government to be too high or unrealistic); and (c) otherwise furnishing information about other offerors' prices. [FAR]

AUDIT The systematic examination of records and documents and/or the securing of other evidence by confirmation, physical inspection, or otherwise, for one or more of the following purposes: determining the propriety or legality of proposed or completed transactions; ascertaining whether all transactions have been recorded and are reflected accurately in accounts; determining the existence of recorded assets and inclusiveness of recorded liabilities; determining the accuracy of financial or statistical statements or reports and the fairness of the facts they represent; determining the degree of compliance with established policies and procedures in terms of financial transactions and business management; and appraising an account system and making recommendations concerning it. [OPM]

AUDITOR A professional accountant acting as a principal advisor to contracting officers on contractor accounting and contract audit matters. [OPM]

AUTHORITY See "Agent Authority."

AUTHORIZATION Funds for programs are authorized by an "authorization act" before the appropriation act is passed. [NC-F]

AUTHORIZATION BILL (1) A bill authorizing the expenditure of public funds. [BLD]

(2) This provides an agency with the legal authority to operate. It recommends policy guidelines and funding levels and must be passed by Congress and signed by the president, but it does not actually provide any money. [DLA]

(3) Congress approves federal programs through passage of an authorization bill. The authorization bill permits an expenditure of money for specific purposes. Congress subsequently appropriates funds out of the Treasury for those purposes. [TIPS(2-6)]

AUTOMATED DATA PROCESSING (ADP) Data processing performed by a system of electronic or electrical machines so interconnected and interacting as to reduce to a minimum the need for human assistance or intervention. [AFIT]

AUTOMATIC DATA PROCESSING EQUIPMENT (ADPE) General purpose, commercially available, mass-produced automatic data processing devices; i.e., components and the equipment systems configured from them, together with commercially available software packages that are provided and are not priced separately, and all documentation relating thereto. [FIRMR]

AVERAGE PROCUREMENT LEAD TIME The average time elapsing between the initiation of procurement actions and the receipt into the system of material purchased as a result of such actions. [AFIT]

AVOIDABLE COSTS Those costs that will not continue if an ongoing operation is changed or deleted. Avoidable costs include department salaries and other costs that could be avoided by not operating the specific department. [MGMT]

AWARD (1) Notification to bidder of acceptance of a bid [or proposal]. [AFIT] (2) The procurement decision to buy a supply or service from a specific concern on specified terms, including dollar amount. [FAI II]

BAILEE In the law of contracts, one to whom goods are bailed; the party to whom personal property is delivered under a contract of bailment. A species of agent to whom something movable is committed in trust for another. [BLD]

BAILMENT The temporary transfer of possession of personal property without a change of ownership for a specific purpose and with the intent that possession will revert to the owner at a later date. [FBL]

Example: The lending of government-owned property to a contractor for the performance of a contract. [OPM]

BASED-ON PRICE A price derived from established catalogue or market prices of commercial items sold in substantial quantities to the general public; the item being purchased must be sufficiently similar to the commercial item to permit the difference between the prices of the items to be identified and justified without resort to cost analysis. [OPM]

BASELINING A process whereby all managers concerned collectively agree on the specific description of the program, requirements, and funding; and make a commitment to manage the program along those guidelines. [DSMC]

BASIC ORDERING AGREEMENT (BOA) An instrument of understanding (not a contract) executed between a procuring activity [buyer] and a contractor [seller] setting forth negotiated contract clauses applicable to future procurements entered into between the parties during the term of the agreement. It includes as specific as possible a description of the supplies or services and a description of the method for determination of prices. [DSMC]

BAYH-DOLE TRADEMARK AMENDMENTS ACT Amended the Stevenson-Wydler Act in order to further assist the process of technology transfer. This Act (P.L. 96-517) allows small businesses and nonprofit organizations to retain title to inventions under government contracts or grants. [TIPS(1-14)]

BEST AND FINAL OFFER (BAFO) A final proposal submission by all offerors in the competitive range submitted at a common cut-off date at the request of the contracting officer after conclusion of negotiations. [NCMA-SS]

BEST VALUE The essential principle of best value is to obtain the best tradeoff between competing factors for a particular purchase requirement. The key to successful best value contracting is (1) consideration of life cycle costs, and (2) marginal analysis, i.e., the use of quantitative as well as qualitative techniques to measure price and technical performance tradeoffs between various proposals. The best value concept applies to acquisitions where price or price-related factors are *not* the primary determinant of who receives the contract award. [TIPS(3-5)]

BID An offer in response to an Invitation for Bids (IFB). [BLD]
See also "Offer."

BID AND PROPOSAL COSTS Costs incurred in preparing, submitting, and supporting bids and proposals (whether or not solicited) on potential government or non-government contracts. [OPM]

BID BOND In government contract administration, an insurance document in which a third party agrees to pay a specific amount of money, if the bonded (insured) bidder fails to sign a contract as bid and accepted by the government. [L&P II]

BID GUARANTEE A form of security accompanying a bid or proposal as assurance that the bidder will not withdraw its bid during the specified time period and will execute a written contract and will furnish such bonds as may be required. [AFIT]

BID OPENING The public announcement of all the bids submitted in response to an Invitation for Bids. [McVay]

BID PROTEST See "Protest."

BID SAMPLE A sample to be furnished by a bidder to show the characteristics of the product offered in the bid. [FAR]

BIDDER One who makes a bid. [BLD]

BIDDERS CONFERENCE See "Pre-bid Conference."

BIDDERS' LIST A list, which is maintained by the procurement office, of contractors and suppliers that have expressed interest in furnishing a specific supply or service to the government. [McVay] Also known as "Bidders' Mailing List."

BILATERAL CONTRACT A contract formed by the exchange of promises in which the promise of one party is consideration supporting the promise of the other. Contrast to "Unilateral Contract," which is formed by the exchange of a promise for an act. [BLD]

BILL OF LADING (1) A document evidencing receipt of goods for shipment issued by a person engaged in the business of transporting for forwarding goods. [BLD]
(2) A carrier's contractual agreement to transport goods from one place to another and to deliver them to a designated person or location for the compensation and under the terms stated in the agreement. [FAI II]

BILL OF MATERIALS (BOM) A descriptive, and quantitative listing of materials, supplies, parts, and components required to produce a designated, complete end-item. [OPM]

BILLING RATE A billing rate is an indirect cost rate (a) established temporarily for interim reimbursement of incurred indirect costs, and (b) adjusted as necessary pending establishment of final indirect cost rates. [FAR]

BLANKET PURCHASE AGREEMENT A method for the government to fill purchase requirements for related supplies, material, equipment, or services by establishing accounts with established sources of supply. Includes certain conditions and provisions that have been negotiated and agreed to in advance; allows the government to make frequent purchases or calls, verbally or in writing, and receive one monthly bill for all supplies or services purchased. [DSMC]

BOARD OF CONTRACT APPEALS A designated administrative tribunal within an executive agency that is authorized to hear, examine, and decide on written requests asking for a change (an appeal) of a contracting officer's decision, and related to a contract made by that agency. [L&P]

BOILERPLATE The name used for printed terms and conditions that are frequently found on the back of purchase order forms in contracts, usually attached as "General Provisions." [Cohen]

BOND A written instrument executed by a bidder or contractor [supplier] (the "principal"), and a second party (the "surety" or "sureties"), to assure fulfillment of the principal's obligations to a third party (the "obligee" or "government"), identified in the bond. If the principal's obligations are not met, the bond assures payment, to the extent stipulated, of any loss sustained by the obligee.

See also "Advance Payment Bond"; "Bid Bond"; "Performance Bond"; and "Payment Bond." [FAR]

BOOK VALUE An accounting term for the value of assets as carried on the books; that is, cost less reserve for depreciation. [BLD]

BOYLE RULE See "Government Contractor Defense."

BRAINSTORMING An idea-gathering technique that uses group interaction to generate many ideas in a short time period. [BOE II]

BRAND NAME DESCRIPTION A purchase description that identifies a product by its brand name and model or part number or other appropriate nomenclature by which the product is offered for sale. [FAR] Frequently specified as "Brand Name or Equal."

BREACH OF CONTRACT The failure, without legal excuse, to perform any promise that forms the whole or part of a contract. *Anticipatory breach* occurs when the promisor, without justification and before he or she has committed a breach, makes a positive statement to the promisee indicating he or she will not or cannot perform his or her contractual duties. [BLD]

BREAKEVEN ANALYSIS The managers of profit-seeking organizations usually study the relationship of revenue (sales), expenses (costs), and net income (net profit). This study is commonly called "Cost-Volume-Profit Analysis." The study of cost-volume-profit relationships is often called "Breakeven Analysis." This term is a misnomer, because the breakeven point is often only incidental to the planning decision at hand. [MGMT]

BREAKEVEN POINT That level of operations where total costs equal total revenue. [NCMA-CA]

BREAKOUT The review of a major weapons system to determine if a particular component may be purchased as a separate item instead of buying it from the weapons system manufacturer. This subsystem would then be provided in the weapons system contract as Government-Furnished Equipment (GFE), rather than Contractor-Furnished Equipment (CFE). [Navy]

BROKER A third party authorized to negotiate with potential vendors for the purchaser, but not authorized to commit the purchaser to the transaction via a contractual document. [Cohen]

BROOKS ACT Enacted in 1965 as P.L. 89-306, this Act established the basic policy for managing data processing equipment in the federal government. The Act authorizes the General Services Administration (GSA) to coordinate and provide for the economic and efficient purchase, lease, and maintenance of automatic data processing equipment. By this Act, GSA was granted exclusive authority to procure Automatic Data Processing Equipment (ADPE), with the power to delegate that authority to federal agencies through Delegations of Procurement Authority (DPAs). [TIPS(3-3)]

BUDGET A plan of action expressed in figures. [NCMA-CA]

BUDGET RESOLUTION Congressional budget committees come up with this legislation, basically an outline, that determines ceilings for the budget authority and outlays for spending. Not legally binding. [DLA]

BUDGET VARIANCE The difference between the amount incurred and the budget figure. [NCMA-CA]

BUDGETED COST FOR WORK PERFORMED (BCWP) The sum of the budgets for completed work packages and completed portions of open work packages. [AFIT]

BUDGETED COST FOR WORK SCHEDULED (BCWS) The sum of the budgets for all work packages and planning packages scheduled to be accomplished (including inprocess work packages). [AFIT]

BULK FUNDING A system whereby a contracting officer receives authorization from a fiscal and accounting officer to obligate funds on purchase documents against a specified lump sum of funds reserved for the purpose and for a specified period of time, rather than obtaining individual obligational authority on each purchase document. [FAR]

BURDEN Also known as "Overhead." See "Overhead."

BURDEN CENTER See "Cost Center."

BUY AMERICAN ACT A federal policy stating that manufactured materials, supplies, or articles acquired for public use shall be substantially constituted from domestically mined or manufactured materials; products are considered to be not of domestic origin if the cost of foreign products used in them accounts for fifty percent of the total cost. [DOD]

BUY-IN The knowing submission of an offer below anticipated cost, with the expectation of increasing the contract amount after award, or receiving follow-on contracts at artificially high prices. [FAR]

BYRD AMENDMENT A common name for P.L. 101-121, Section 219, which instructed OMB to issue government-wide guidance restricting the use of public funds to pay for lobbying. The guidelines define lobbying as influencing or attempting to influence any agency employee, member of Congress, or congressional staff member in connection with the award, renewal extension, or modification of any federal contract. Companies must file compliance certifications disclosing any outside personnel it hires, or expects to hire, with private funds. [TIPS(1-6)]

CAPITAL An economist uses the term "Capital" to mean all the man-made aids used in production. Sometimes called "Investment Goods," capital consists of machinery, tools, buildings, transportation and distribution facilities, and inventories of unfinished goods. A basic characteristic of capital goods is that they are used to produce other goods. [ECON]

CAPITAL, COST OF Under the net-present-value method, a manager determines some minimum desired rate of return. The minimum rate is often called "Cost of Capital." All expected future cash flows are discounted to the present, using this minimum desired rate. If the result is zero or positive, the project is desirable, and if negative, it is undesirable. [MGMT]

CAPITAL EQUIPMENT For accounting purposes, most firms classify capital equipment as noncurrent assets, which are capitalized and depreciated over the course of their economic lives. The purchase of a particular piece of capital equipment typically occurs only once every five to ten years or so. A unique feature of most capital equipment purchases is the lead time requirements. Manufacturing lead time is usually a matter of months or years. An expenditure of funds for capital equipment is an investment. If purchased wisely and operated efficiently, capital equipment generates profit for its owner. The purchase of most major equipment involves the expenditure of a substantial sum of money. [DBL]

CARDINAL CHANGE (1) A major change to a contract that is made outside the scope of the contract and is, therefore, unenforceable by the government. [McVay]
(2) Contract change having the effect of making the work as performed not essentially the same work as the parties bargained for when the contract was awarded, and thus constituting a breach of contract by the government. [GUIDE]

CASH FLOW (1) The cash generated from the property. It is different than net income; cash flow looks to the amount left after all payments are made, whether they are tax deductible or not. Also defined as cash receipts minus disbursements from a given asset, or group of assets, for a given period. [BLD]
(2) The net effect of cash receipts and disbursements. [NCMA-CA]

CAUSE AND EFFECT DIAGRAM A structured form of brainstorming that graphically shows the relationship of causes and subcauses to an identified effect (problem). See also "Fishbone Diagram." [BOE II]

CEILING See "Adjusted Ceiling" and "Negotiated Ceiling."

CENTRAL PROCUREMENT ACTIVITY A level of government contracting activity in which assignments are performed by formal contracting and involve procurements up to major components of agency critical programs and facilities, and the equipment to support these programs. Also includes coordinated interdepartmental, and government-wide commodity assignments, as well as area-wide support responsibilities. [OPM]

CENTRALIZATION OF PURCHASING Centralization exists when the entire purchasing function is made the responsibility of a single person. This person is held accountable by top management for proper performance of purchasing activities. When functioning properly, centralized purchasing produces the following benefits: duplication is minimized; volume discounts are possible; transportation savings can be realized; purchasing specialists can buy more efficiently due to their expertise;

suppliers can offer better prices because their administrative costs are reduced; more effective inventory control is possible; fewer orders are processed for the same quantity of goods; and management control is facilitated. [DBL]

CERTIFICATE OF APPOINTMENT The document that empowers a person to act on the behalf of the government as a contracting officer. [McVay] See also "Warrant."

CERTIFICATE OF COMPETENCY The certificate issued by the Small Business Administration stating that the holder is responsible (with respect to all elements of responsibility) for the purpose of receiving and performing a specific government contract. [FAR]

CERTIFICATE OF CURRENT COST OR PRICING DATA (1) A document submitted by the contractor attesting that the cost or pricing data provided to the government were accurate, complete, and current as of the date negotiations were completed. [McVay]

(2) Prescribed certificate required to be executed by contractors that must submit certified cost or pricing data under the Truth in Negotiations Act (TINA). [GUIDE]

CERTIFICATION OF A CLAIM The requirement, under the Contract Disputes Act, that contract claims over $50,000 be accompanied by a statement that simultaneously asserts that the claim is made in good faith, that supporting data is accurate and complete, and that the amount requested reflects the contract adjustment believed due. [GUIDE]

CHANGE IN SCOPE Change to approved program requirements or specifications after negotiation of a basic contract. It may result in an increase or decrease. [AFIT]

CHANGE ORDER A written order signed by the contracting officer or buyer, authorized by contract clause, to modify contractual requirements within the scope of the contract. [OPM]

CHANGE PROPOSAL See "Engineering Change Proposal."

CHANGES CLAUSE A standard clause in government contracts. There are several versions corresponding to the specific type of contract, but all have certain common characteristics. The clause,

mandatory for most government contracts, provides a contractual grant of authority to the government by its supplier. It gives the government the right to alter unilaterally specific matters affecting the performance of the contract. [Sherman]

CHRISTIAN DOCTRINE Based on an actual court case, a principle that maintains that if a significant clause is required to be included in a government contract, the contract will be read to include it, even though the clause is not physically incorporated in the document. [NC-F]

CIVILIAN AGENCY ACQUISITION COUNCIL (CAAC) Group, composed of members from federal civilian agencies, that has joint responsibility with the Defense Acquisition Regulatory Council for revision of the Federal Acquisition Regulation. [GUIDE] See also "Defense Acquisition Regulatory Council."

CLAIM A written demand or written assertion by one of the contracting parties seeking, as a matter of right, the payment of money in a sum certain, the adjustment or interpretation of the contract terms, or other relief arising under or relating to the contract. A claim arising under a contract, unlike a claim relating to that contract, is a claim that can be resolved under a contract clause that provides for the relief sought by the claimant. A voucher, invoice, or other routine request for payment that is not in dispute when submitted is not a claim. The submission is not a claim. The submission may be converted to a claim, by written notice to the contracting officer. [FAR]

CLAIM CERTIFICATION See "Certification of a Claim."

CLAIMS COURT See "United States Court of Claims."

CLARIFICATION A communication in negotiations for the sole purpose of eliminating minor irregularities, informalities, or apparent clerical mistakes in a proposal. [FAR]

CLAUSE A term or condition used in contracts or in both solicitations and contracts, and applying after contract award or both before and after award. Clauses state the rights and obligations of the parties to a contract. [FAI]

CLAYTON ACT A federal law (15 U.S.C.A. 12-27) enacted in 1914 as an amendment to the Sherman Antitrust Act dealing with antitrust regulations and unfair trade practices. The Act prohibits price discrimination, tying and exclusive dealing contracts, mergers, and interlocking directorates, where the effect may be substantially to lessen competition or tend to create a monopoly in any line of commerce. [BLD]

CLOSED CONTRACT A contract on which all contractor and government obligations and administrative actions have been completed. [AFIT]

CLOSEOUT The process of declaring that the obligations under a contract have been satisfied and that a procurement file is both physically and administratively complete. A closeout can occur when (1) the contractor's supplies or services have been accepted and paid for, and (2) all documentation on the procurement is finalized and properly assembled. [FAI II]

CLOSING DATE The last day on which proposals or quotations will be accepted. [NCMA-SB]

CODE OF FEDERAL REGULATIONS (CFR) Official codification of United States administrative regulations. [GUIDE] The Federal Acquisition Regulation (FAR) is Title 48 of the CFR, and is thus part of the CFR.

CO-DEVELOPMENT A development project to which more than one government contributes efforts or resources. [MSA]

COLLUSION Any understanding or agreement, expressed, implied, formal, or informal, among bidders or competitors concerning bids or proposals for the sale of products or services; disclosure of a bid or proposal by a bidder to any other bidder or competitor prior to the official opening of all bids or proposals; any attempt to induce a competitor not to submit a bid or proposal. [BOE]

COLOR OF MONEY A term used to describe the type of procurement money used for a particular item. Different kinds of appropriated funds must be used for various procurements, e.g., RDT&E (Research, Development, Test and Evaluation), O&M (Operations and Maintenance), and FMS (Foreign Military Sales). [Navy]

COMMERCE BUSINESS DAILY The official government publication used to announce business opportunities pertaining to the procurement and sale of supplies and services. It contains announcements of procurement actions, contract awards, and subcontracting opportunities, and is published by the Department of Commerce. [FAI II]

COMMERCIAL AND GOVERNMENT ENTITY (CAGE) CODE An identification code that provides a government agency the following information about a firm: name, address, socioeconomic data, and type of business, i.e., manufacturer or regular dealer. A firm needs only one code. [Foglia]

COMMERCIAL ITEM An item, including both supplies and services, of a class or kind that is regularly used for other than government purposes and is sold or traded in the course of conducting normal business operations. [OPM] See also "Non-Developmental Item" and "Off-the-Shelf."

COMMERCIAL-OFF-THE-SHELF (COTS) See "Off-the-Shelf."

COMMERCIAL SALE Sale made by U.S. industry directly to a foreign buyer that is not administered by the Department of Defense through Foreign Military Sales (FMS) procedures. [MSA]

COMMERCIAL-TYPE ITEMS Any items, including those expended or consumed in use which, in addition to military use, are used and traded in normal civilian enterprise, and which are, or can be, imported/exported through normal international trade channels. [MSA]

COMMISSION ON GOVERNMENT PROCUREMENT (COGP) In 1969, P.L. 91-129 established the Commission. The COGP was a group of twelve members, representing Congress, the executive branch, and the public. The Comptroller General was made a statutory member. The COGP report released in December 1972 contained 149 recommendations for improvements of the federal procurement process. Among the recommendations were establishment of an independent, centralized office for government-wide procurement policy matters, a federal procurement institute for the uniform training and development of government procurement personnel, and a single uniform procurement system for all government agencies. [Culver]

COMMON COST See "Joint Cost."

COMMON LAW Written or unwritten laws that have evolved through custom and usage (from English common law) without written legislation. [FBL]

COMMONALITY A quality applying to material or systems possessing like and interchangeable characteristics enabling each to be utilized or operated and maintained by personnel trained on the others without additional specialized training. Also, having interchangeable repair parts and/or components, and applying to consumable items interchangeably equivalent without adjustment. [DSMC]

COMPENSABLE DELAYS A delay for which the government is contractually responsible that excuses the contractor's failure to perform and is compensable. Suspension of Work (FAR 52.212-12) and Stop Work (FAR 52.212-13) and Government Delay of Work (FAR 52.212-15) are examples of compensable delays. [FAR]

COMPENSATION CLAUSE Also sometimes called "Payment." This clause sets out the amount payable under the contract, supporting data required to be furnished with invoices, and other payment terms, such as time for payment and retention. Depending on the complexity of the contract, these areas may be individually addressed in separate clauses. [Cohen]

COMPETITION Part of an acquisition strategy whereby more than one contractor is sought to bid on performing a service or function, with the winner being selected on the basis of criteria established by the activity for whom the work is to be performed. [DSMC]

COMPETITION ADVOCATE A position established by the Competition in Contracting Act of 1984. Each agency is required to have a competition advocate who, in turn, designates a competition advocate for each procuring activity of the agency. The competition advocate is responsible for promoting full and open competition and for challenging any barriers to such competition. [Navy]

COMPETITION IN CONTRACTING ACT (CICA) A 1984 congressional act designed to foster competition and promote cost savings; requires the use of advance procurement planning and market research, as well as the use of commercial products whenever practicable. [FAR]

COMPETITIVE NEGOTIATION A procurement involving (1) a Request for Proposal that states the government's requirements and criteria for evaluation, (2) the submission of timely proposals by a maximum number of offerors, (3) discussions with those offerors found to be within the competitive range, and (4) award of a contract to the one offeror whose offer, price, and other consideration factors are most advantageous to the government. [OPM]

COMPETITIVE RANGE A range of acceptable standards, determined by the contracting officer on the basis of price, cost, or technical factors; the contracting officer must conduct written or oral discussions with all responsible offerors that submit proposals within this range. [OPM]

COMPETITIVE TIME See "Uncompensated Overtime."

COMPONENT BREAKOUT An acquisition strategy to convert some items, usually parts or self-contained elements of a complete operating equipment end item, from contractor-furnished to government-procured items. [L&P II]

COMPTROLLER GENERAL The head of the General Accounting Office. [TIPS(3-4)]

COMPUTER-AIDED ACQUISITION AND LOGISTICS SUPPORT (CALS) A Department of Defense (DOD) initiative that mandates electronic interchange between contractors and government agencies of technical information, documents, and support information, including cost and schedule details, using Electronic Data Interchange (EDI). [EDIW(1-11)]

COMPUTER-AIDED DESIGN/COMPUTER-AIDED MANUFACTURING (CAD/CAM) (1) CAD/CAM systems are a computerized means of providing standardization in the predesign stage in order to facilitate data transfer between CAD systems of different manufacturers and for transfers between CAD and CAM systems. [DBL]

(2) CAD/CAM represents a new wave of Electronic Data Interchange (EDI) technology that helps improve the speed and quality of manufacturing processes. For example, two engineering teams located miles apart cooperate on a design by moving the needed drawings back and forth electronically, altering schematics on their computer screens. Together, they design an intricate part that can be efficiently manufactured to satisfy the customer's requirements. [EDIW(2-1)]

CONCERTED REFUSALS TO DEAL Agreements or understandings by which two or more companies jointly refuse to do business with a specific third party. [BOE]

CONCURRENT INSPECTION Judgment of product or procedural acceptability conducted concurrently by the contractor's inspection personnel and the government's quality assurance personnel. [AFIT]

CONFIGURATION A collection of an item's descriptive and governing characteristics that can be expressed in functional terms (what performance the item is expected to achieve) and in physical terms (what the item should look like and consist of when it is built). [DSMC]

CONFIGURATION MANAGEMENT A procedure for applying technical and administrative direction and surveillance to identify and document the functional and physical characteristics of an item or system; control any changes to such characteristics; and record and report the change, process, and implementation status. The configuration management process must be carefully tailored to the capacity, size, scope, phase of the life cycle, and nature and complexity of the system involved. [DSMC]

CONFLICT OF INTEREST Term used in connection with public officials and fiduciaries and their relationship to matters of private interest or gain to them. Ethical problems connected therewith are covered by statutes in most jurisdictions and by federal statutes on the federal level. A conflict of interest arises when an employee's personal or financial interest conflicts or appears to conflict with his or her official responsibility. [BLD2]

CONSENSUS DECISION A decision made after all aspects of an issue, both positive and negative, have been brought out to the extent that everyone openly understands and supports the decision and the reasons for making it. [BOE II]

CONSEQUENTIAL DAMAGES Those costs that result from a particular cause. For example, a product failure may mean that the purchaser has incurred not only the added cost necessary to replace the product, but has also lost income that would have resulted had the product not failed. The lost income would be a consequential damage. The extent to which consequential damages may be recovered depends on the language contained in the contract and the law in a particular jurisdiction. [Cohen]

CONSERVATISM An accounting convention that provides guidance for accountants where solutions to uncertain elements should be chosen on the basis that would least likely overstate assets and income. Historically, this has been the most pervasive approach that accountants have used in preparing financial statements. [NCMA-CA]

CONSIDERATION Anything of value that changes hands between the parties to a contract. [FAI]

CONSIGNEE A person, group of persons, or organization receiving supplies and services and that is named on the bill of lading. [FAI II]

CONSISTENCY An accounting principle that is vital in order to provide comparable financial information to interested users from period to period. Financial statements would not provide meaningful information if the accounting treatment of financial data changed continuously over a span of time. The consistency principle is designed to achieve comparability between accounting periods. Any changes in accounting treatment that may occur should be reported and the effects of the change disclosed. [NCMA-CA]

CONSOLIDATED LIST OF DEBARRED, SUSPENDED, AND INELIGIBLE CONTRACTORS A single, comprehensive listing prepared by the

General Services Administration, of business firms and individuals debarred, suspended, or otherwise excluded by government agencies from receiving government contracts. [DOD]
CONSTANT YEAR DOLLARS Level of costs, without inflation, in a specified base year. [Navy]
CONSTRAINTS Restrictions or boundary conditions that impact overall capability, priority, and resources in system acquisition. [DSMC]
CONSTRUCTIVE That which is established by the mind of the law in its act of construing facts, conduct, circumstances, or instruments. That which has not the character assigned to it in its own essential nature, but acquires such character in consequence of the way in which it is regarded by a rule or policy of law; hence, inferred, implied, or made out by legal interpretation. (The word "legal" is sometimes used here in lieu of "constructive.") [BLD]
CONSTRUCTIVE ACCELERATION A requirement (based on the reasonable interpretation of the words, acts, or inaction of authorized government employees) that a contractor complete its work by a date earlier than one that would reflect the time extensions to which it is entitled because of excusable delays. [GUIDE]
CONSTRUCTIVE CHANGE An oral or written act or omission by an authorized government official that is of such a nature that it is construed to have the same effect as a written change order. [OPM]
CONSULTANT An individual or firm retained for the specialized expertise it possesses. [Cohen]
CONSULTING SERVICES Consulting services are those services of a purely advisory nature relating to the governmental functions of agency administration and management and program management. [FAR]
CONTINGENCY A possible future event or condition arising from presently known or suspected causes, the cost of outcome of which is indeterminable at the present time. [OPM]
CONTINGENT FEE Any commission, percentage, brokerage, or other fee that is contingent upon the success that a

person or concern has in securing a government contract. [FAR]
CONTINUING RESOLUTION If the appropriations bill has not been signed by the beginning of the fiscal year, this legislation allows an agency to continue operating at the previous year's spending level. The resolution has a set expiration date. [DLA]
CONTINUOUS QUALITY IMPROVEMENT The concept that nothing is perfect, and that all work processes are grounds for constant evaluation and potential improvement. [BOE II]
CONTRA PROFERENTUM Used in connection with the construction of written documents to the effect that an ambiguous provision is construed most strongly against the person who selected the language. [BLD]
CONTRACT An agreement, enforceable by law, between two or more competent parties to do or not do something not prohibited by law, for legal consideration. Involves both an offer and an acceptance. [PW]
CONTRACT ADMINISTRATION The oversight of a contractor's [supplier's] performance pursuant to the fulfillment of the terms, conditions, and specifications of a contract. [OPM]
CONTRACT ADMINISTRATION OFFICE The activity identified in the DOD Directory of Contract Administration Services Components assigned to perform contract administration responsibilities. It is a general term and includes ARPROs, AFPROs, NAVPROs, SUPSHIPs, and DCAS field offices. [OPM]
CONTRACT AUDIT The evaluation of the accuracy and propriety of contractors' cost representations and claims by the review and analysis of contractors' and subcontractors' policies, systems and controls; includes examination of books, accounts, basic records, and operations. [AFIT]
CONTRACT AWARD Takes place when contracting officer [buyer] has signed and distributed the contract to the contractor [seller]. [DSMC]
CONTRACT BOND A guarantee backed by cash or other security, of the faithful performance and fulfillment of the undertakings, covenants, terms, and

conditions contained in a contract. [AFIT]

CONTRACT CHANGE PROPOSAL (CCP) See "Engineering Change Proposal."

CONTRACT CLAIM Any request for relief, adjustment, or consideration by a party to the contract for an act which, in the opinion of the claimant, is not within the scope or intent of the original contract. [OPM]

CONTRACT CLOSEOUT See "Closeout."

CONTRACT COST The aggregate dollar amount paid to the contractor [supplier]. [AFIT]

CONTRACT DATA REQUIREMENTS LIST (CDRL) Document used to order [buy] and require delivery of data; it tells the contractor what data to deliver, when and how such data will be accepted, where to look for instructions, etc. [DSMC]

CONTRACT DISPUTES ACT In 1978, the Contract Disputes Act (41 U.S.C. 601-613) established procedures and requirements for asserting and resolving claims by or against contractors arising under or relating to a contract subject to the Act. The Act provides for payment of interest on contractor claims in excess of $50,000, and for a civil penalty for contractor claims that are fraudulent or based on a misrepresentation of fact. [FAR]

CONTRACT INTERPRETATION The entire process of determining what the parties agreed to in their bargain. The basic objective of contract interpretation is to determine the intent of the parties. Rules calling for interpretation of the document *against* the drafter, and imposing a duty to seek clarification on the contractor, allocate risks of contractual ambiguities by resolving disputes in favor of the party least responsible for the ambiguity. [NC-A]

CONTRACT MANAGEMENT REVIEW An appraisal of the effectiveness of local offices' interpretation and application of policies, directives, and procedures, and of the capability of field activities to comply with them. [OPM]

CONTRACT MODIFICATION Any written alteration in the specification, delivery point, rate of delivery, contract period, price, quantity, or other provision of an existing contract, accomplished in accordance with a contract clause; may be unilateral or bilateral. [OPM]

See also "Change Order" and "Supplemental Agreement."

CONTRACT PRICING PROPOSAL The instrument required of an offeror for the submission or identification of cost or pricing data, by which an offeror submits to the government a summary of estimated (or incurred) costs suitable for detailed review and analysis. [OPM]

CONTRACT REQUIREMENTS In addition to specified performance requirements, contract requirements include those defined in the Statement of Work (SOW); specifications, standards and related documents; the Contract Data Requirements List (CDRL); management systems; and contract terms and conditions. [OPM]

CONTRACT SCHEDULE The complete statement of the requirement in the solicitation, including not only the Statement of Work and Specifications, but also the terms and conditions with respect to packaging and marking, inspection and acceptance, deliveries or performance, contract administration data, and other special contract requirements. The Schedule includes Sections A through H of the Uniform Contract Format. [FAI]

See also "Uniform Contract Format."

CONTRACT TYPE A specific pricing arrangement employed for the performance of work under the contract. [OPM]

See also "Cost-Plus-Award-Fee Contract"; "Cost-Plus-Fixed-Fee Contract"; "Cost-Plus-Incentive-Fee Contract"; "Firm-Fixed-Price Contract"; "Fixed-Price-Incentive Contract"; and "Fixed-Price Redeterminable Contract."

CONTRACT WORK HOURS AND SAFETY STANDARDS ACT Requires that certain contracts contain a clause (See FAR 52.222-4) specifying that no laborer or mechanic doing any part of the work contemplated by the contract shall be required or permitted to work more than 40 hours in any workweek unless paid for all additional hours at not less than 1-1/2 times the basic rate of pay. [FAR]

CONTRACTING The entire spectrum of action associated with obtaining supplies or services, from initial description through solicitation and contract award and all phases of contract administration. [NCMA-SS]

CONTRACTING ACTIVITY An element of an agency that is designated by the agency head and to which is delegated broad authority regarding acquisition functions. [NCMA-SS]

CONTRACTING OFFICE An office that prepares solicitations and awards or executes a contract for supplies or services and performs postaward functions not assigned to a contract administration office. [NCMA-SS]

CONTRACTING OFFICER The only person with the authority to obligate government funds and enter into, administer, and/or terminate contracts; also applies to any authorized representatives of the contracting officer acting within their limits of delegated authority. [OPM]

CONTRACTING OFFICER'S TECHNICAL REPRESENTATIVE (COTR) A person provided to assist the contracting officer in matters related to inspection, acceptance, and other duties; a person without specific authority acting as an extension of the contracting officer at a specific duty station. [OPM]

CONTRACTING OUT The process by which a government activity contracts with private enterprise, as opposed to performing work in-house, for commercial or industrial products or services. [OPM]

CONTRACTOR A supplier, vendor, or manufacturer having a contract (commitment) to provide specific supplies or services. [FAI II]

CONTRACTOR COST DATA REPORT A contractual report that provides a consistent, disciplined, historical data base for use in cost estimate/cost analysis studies. [AFIT]

CONTRACTOR FINANCING The provision of capital to a contractor through equity capital, private financing, customary progress payments, guaranteed loans, unusual progress payments, or advance payments. [OPM]

CONTRACTOR-OWNED, CONTRACTOR-OPERATED (COCO) A manufacturing facility owned and operated by a private contractor performing a service, under contract, for the government. [AFIT]

CONTRACTOR PURCHASING SYSTEM REVIEW (CPSR) An annual government audit of contractor management systems for contractors whose sales to the government exceed, or are anticipated to exceed, $10 million. [NCMA-SC]

CONTRACTOR RISK ASSESSMENT GUIDE (CRAG) A DOD program that proposes to cut oversight if industry strengthens its own internal controls. Contractors that can demonstrate the implementation of internal control systems that meet CRAG control objectives will receive less direct government oversight. Control measures have been established for five identified "high-risk" areas for government contracting:
* indirect cost submissions;
* labor charging;
* material management and accounting systems;
* estimating systems; and
* purchasing. [TIPS(3-2)]

CONTROL CHART A chart showing sequential or time-related performance of a process that is used to determine when the process is operating in or out of statistical control, using control limits defined on the chart. [BOE II]

CONTROL LIMITS A statistically derived limit for a process that indicates the spread of variations attributable to chance variation in the process. Control limits are based on averages. [BOE II]

CONVENIENCE TERMINATION Right reserved to the government, under the standard Termination for Convenience of the Government clause, to bring an end to contracts that are made obsolete by technological and other developments, or that are otherwise no longer advantageous to the government. [GUIDE]
   See also "Termination."

CONVENTIONAL ARMS TRANSFER The transfer of nonnuclear weapons, aircraft, equipment, and military services from supplier states to recipient states. The U.S. has viewed arms transfers as a useful foreign policy instrument to strengthen collective defense arrangements, maintain regional military balances, secure U.S. bases, and compensate for the withdrawal of troops. U.S. arms are transferred by grants as in the Military Assistance Program (MAP), by private commercial sales, and by government-to-government sales under foreign military sales (FMS). [MSA]

COOPERATIVE AGREEMENT Cooperative agreements and grants are a means of providing federal assistance. The cooperative agreement differs from the grant because the sponsoring federal agency is involved, collaboratively, in management of the undertaking, and because cooperative agreements are often established with private enterprise organizations. Such agreements may provide for sharing the cost as well as the management of the undertaking. [Sherman3]
  See also "Federal Assistance" and "Grant."

COOPERATIVE DEVELOPMENT Any method by which governments cooperate to make better use of their collective research and development resources to include technical information exchange, harmonizing of requirements, codevelopment, interdependent research and development, and agreement on standards. Many of these elements occur prior to appointment of the program manager or occur outside the program management environment, but their results impact programs that have multinational involvement. [DOD-MMH]

COOPERATIVE PURCHASING A process whereby two or more communities, counties, or other governmental jurisdictions voluntarily agree to coordinate their purchases of one or more commodities to obtain the best unit price through volume buying. [Steinhauer]

COPELAND ACT The law that prohibits kickbacks on construction contracts financed by the government. [McVay]
  Also known as "Anti-Kickback Act."

COPRODUCTION, INTERNATIONAL Method by which items intended for military application are produced and/or assembled under the provisions of a cooperative agreement that requires the transfer of technical information and know-how from one nation to another. [MSA]

COPYRIGHT A royalty-free, nonexclusive, and irrevocable license to reproduce, translate, publish, use, and dispose of written or recorded material, and to authorize others to do so. Usually valid for 17-year periods. [UNI]

COST The amount of money expended in acquiring a product or obtaining a service, or the total of acquisition costs, plus all expenses related to operating and maintaining an item once acquired. [ASPM]

COST ACCOUNT A management control point at which actual costs can be accumulated and compared to budgeted cost of work performed. A cost account is a natural control point for cost/schedule planning and control, since it represents the work assigned to one responsible organizational element on one contract Work Breakdown Structure (WBS) element. [JIG]

COST ACCOUNTING A system of accounting analysis and reporting on production costs of goods or services, on operation costs of programs, activities, functions, or organizational units; includes cost estimating, determination of cost standards based on engineering data, and/or comparison of actual and standard costs for the purpose of aiding cost control. [OPM]
  Also known as "Management Accounting" and "Managerial Accounting."

COST ACCOUNTING STANDARDS Federal standards designed to provide a consistency and coherency in defense and other government contract accounting. [FAR]

COST ACCOUNTING STANDARDS BOARD (CASB) Established in 1969 as an agency of the U.S. Congress to promote uniformity and consistency of cost accounting rules and regulations for government contractors. This led to the development of Cost Accounting Standards (CAS), which formally became a matter of policy when the Federal Acquisition Regulation (FAR) Council incorporated the nineteen CAS into the FAR at Part 30. Congress discontinued funding for the CASB in 1980, whereupon the Board ceased to exist. In 1988, P.L. 100-679 permanently reauthorized the Office of Federal Procurement Policy (OFPP). In addition, the law reconstituted CASB within the OFPP. It also mandated that the CAS be mandatory for all executive agencies, not just DOD as previously. [NCMA-CA]

COST ANALYSIS The review and evaluation of a contractor's costs or pricing data, and of the judgmental factors applied in projecting from the data to the estimated costs, for the purpose of determining the degree to which the contractor's proposed costs represent what contract performance should cost, assuming reasonable economy and efficiency. [OPM]

COST CENTER (1) The smallest unit of activity or area of responsibility for which costs are accumulated. [NCMA-CA] (2) Any subdivision of an organization comprised of workers, equipment areas, activities, or combination of these that is established for the purpose of assigning or allocating costs. Cost centers are also used as a base for performance standards. Also known as "Burden Center" and "Cost Pool." [DOD-MMH]

COST CONTRACT A cost-reimbursement contract that provides no fee. [L&P II]

COST ESTIMATING The process of forecasting a future result in terms of cost, based upon information available at the time. [ASPM]

COST OBJECTIVE A function, organizational subdivision, contract, or other work unit for which cost data are desired and for which provision is made to accumulate and measure the cost of processes, products, jobs, capitalized projects, etc. [FAR]

COST OF CAPITAL See "Capital, Cost of."

COST OF GOODS SOLD Inventoriable costs released to the current period (an expense) as a result of the sale of goods. [NCMA-CA]

COST OR PRICING DATA All verifiable facts that could reasonably have a significant effect on price negotiations and are available at the time of agreement on price. [OPM]

COST OVERRUN A net change in contractual amount beyond that contemplated by a contract target price (FPI contract), estimated cost plus fee (any cost reimbursable contract), or redeterminable price (FPR contract), due to the contractor's actual costs being over target or anticipated contract costs. [OPM]

COST PERFORMANCE REPORT A monthly report procured by the government Program Manager (PM) from the contractor to obtain data from the contractor's management system. In standard format and used in the PM's decision-making process. [DSMC]

COST-PLUS-AWARD-FEE (CPAF) CONTRACT A cost-reimbursement type of contract with special incentive fee provisions used to provide motivation for excellence in contract performance in such areas as quality, timeliness, ingenuity, and cost effectiveness. [OPM]

COST-PLUS-FIXED-FEE (CPFF) CONTRACT A cost-reimbursement type of contract that provides for the payment of a fixed fee to the contractor. Does not vary with actual costs, but may be adjusted as a result of any subsequent changes in the work or services to be performed under the contract. [OPM]

COST-PLUS-INCENTIVE-FEE (CPIF) CONTRACT A cost-reimbursement type of contract with provision for a fee that is adjusted by a formula in accordance with the relationship between total allowable costs and target costs. [OPM]

COST-PLUS-PERCENTAGE-OF-COST (CPPC) CONTRACT An outlawed contract type that bases the contractor's fee on the amount of funds it expends. [McVay]

COST POOL See "Cost Center."

COST PRINCIPLES The regulations that establish rules and policies relating to the general treatment of costs in government contracts, particularly the allowability of costs. [GUIDE]

COST-REIMBURSEMENT CONTRACT A form of pricing arrangement that provides for payment of allowable, allocable, and reasonable costs incurred in the performance of a contract to the extent that such costs are prescribed or permitted by the contract. [OPM]

See also "Cost-Plus-Award-Fee Contract"; "Cost-Plus-Fixed-Fee Contract"; "Cost-Plus-Incentive-Fee Contract"; and "Cost-Sharing Contract."

COST RISK An assumption of possible monetary loss or gain in light of the job or work to be done; an element to be considered in the negotiation of a fair and reasonable price, as well as in the determination of contract type. [OPM]

COST/SCHEDULE CONTROL SYSTEMS CRITERIA (C/SCSC) Standards used to evaluate the effectiveness of contractors' internal systems. The C/SCSC does not require any data to be reported to the government, but does provide for access to data needed to evaluate the system and monitor its operation during the life of the contract. [DSMC]

COST-SHARING CONTRACT A cost-reimbursement contract in which the contractor receives no fee and is reimbursed only for an agreed-upon portion of its allowable costs. [FAR]

COST-TYPE CONTRACT Also known as "Cost-Reimbursement Contract." See "Cost-Reimbursement Contract."

COST-VOLUME-PROFIT ANALYSIS See "Breakeven Analysis."

COUNTEROFFER (1) The nonacceptance of the government's offer to buy as presented. A counteroffer introduces a new condition, item, quantity, or quality, or it varies from the original terms in the government's offer. Counteroffers by suppliers under sealed-bid procedures are rejected. However, under negotiated procedures (including small purchases), counteroffers are permissible and may be negotiated, e.g., a purchase order is only an offer to buy, and the terms of acceptance may be negotiated. [FAI II]

(2) A counterproposal different from an offer that an offeree makes in response to the offer. In making a counteroffer, the offeree rejects the previous offer. [FBL]

COURT OF CLAIMS See "United States Court of Claims."

CRITICAL DEPENDENCIES The interrelationships existing within or among processes that are primary drivers of defects or errors in a product or service. [BOE II]

CRITICAL DESIGN REVIEW (CDR) Determines that the detail design satisfies the performance and engineering specialty requirements of the development; that the specification establishes the detail design compatibility among the item and other items of equipment facilities, computer programs, and personnel; that the detail design assesses producibility and risk areas; and that it reviews the preliminary product specifications. [DOD-MMH]

CRITICAL ITEM A subsystem, component, material, or other item that could seriously jeopardize the successful completion of program requirements if not available when required during the procurement/production. Also, an item that could have an adverse impact on cost, schedule, quality, and/or technical performance specifications. [DSMC]

CRITICAL PATH METHOD (CPM) One of the best known (along with the Program Evaluation and Review Technique, or PERT) techniques derived from the basic critical path scheduling concept. CPM was originally developed in 1955 by the du Pont and Remington Rand companies for use in coping with complex plant maintenance problems. In practice, the application of CPM/PERT generally is accomplished with a computer program. It uses network diagrams to show time and dependency relationships between the activities that make up the total project. The purpose of the technique is to keep all the "parts" arriving on schedule so that the total project can be completed as planned. [DBL]

CRITICAL PATH SCHEDULING A tool that can be used to manage project buying activities, construction projects, and research and development projects, etc. The critical path approach quantifies information about uncertainties faced by the activities responsible for meeting a predetermined time schedule. The very process of analyzing these uncertainties focuses the manager's attention on the most critical series of activities in the total project—those that constitute the critical path. A variety of specific techniques have been derived from the basic critical path scheduling concept. The best known of these are "Critical Path Method (CPM)" and "Program Evaluation and Review Technique (PERT)." [DBL]

CRITICAL SUBCONTRACT A subcontract, the failure of which seriously jeopardizes the successful completion of a program within cost, schedule, quality, and/or technical performance specifications. [DSMC]

CRITICAL SUCCESS FACTORS Indicators developed by a customer that indicate the defect-fee character of a product or service. [BOE II]

CUMULATIVE DISCOUNT See "Quantity Discount."

CURE NOTICE A notice sent by the contracting officer stating that the contractor will be subject to a default termination unless it corrects a specific contract noncompliance or makes necessary progress to meet the delivery schedule. [NCMA-SC]
See also "Default Termination."

CURRENT YEAR DOLLARS Level of cost, with inflation, in the year that actual cost will be incurred. [Navy]
Also known as "Then-year Dollars."

CUSTOMER Anyone for whom an organization provides goods or services. [BOE II]

DATA DOCUMENTATION COSTS Costs of converting source data to the documents prescribed in the contract for delivery to the government. [AFIT]

DATA REQUIREMENTS REVIEW BOARD A board appointed by a responsible manager to assist and advise in the determination of data requirements. [AFIT]

DATA RIGHTS CLAUSE The data rights issue involves the complicated question of who owns the rights to data developed under a contract. The answer lies in the contract provisions that have been negotiated between the parties. There are three commonly used means of protecting data in the commercial world: trade secret status, copyright protection, and patent provisions. Federal government contracting has four types of rights the government can obtain for use of data developed under federal contracts: unlimited rights, limited rights, restricted rights (which apply only to computer software), and government purpose license rights. [NES92]

DATA SHEET See "Financial Accounting Data Sheet."

DAVIS BACON ACT A statute that requires all laborers and mechanics employed on federally funded construction, alteration, or repair contracts be paid the locally prevailing wage rate (as determined by the Secretary of Labor). [McVay]

DEBARMENT Action taken by a debarring official to exclude a contractor from government contracting and subcontracting for a reasonable, specified period. The following are some causes for debarment per FAR 9.406-2: conviction of or civil judgment for any offense indicating a lack of business integrity (fraud, antitrust violations, theft, bribery, etc.); violation of the terms of a government contract so serious as to justify debarment; violations of the Drug-Free Workplace Act of 1988; or any other cause of so serious or compelling a nature that it affects the present responsibility of a government contractor or subcontractor. [FAR]

DEBRIEF An explanation given by government personnel to an offeror detailing the reasons its proposal was unsuccessful. [McVay]

DECENTRALIZATION OF PURCHASING This occurs when personnel from other functional areas—production, engineering, marketing, finance, etc.—decide on sources of supply, negotiate with vendors directly, or perform any of the other major functions of purchasing. Three types of situations justify some decentralization: companies that process single natural raw materials; technically oriented firms that are heavily involved in research; and, operation of multisite institutional and manufacturing organizations. The purchase of nontechnical odds and ends also often calls for a partial decentralization of purchasing. [DBL]

DECISION SUPPORT SYSTEMS A type of expert system. [TIPS(2-8)]
See also "Expert System."

DEDUCTIVE CHANGE A change resulting in a reduction in contract price because of a net reduction in the contractor's work. [GUIDE]

DEFAULT (1) The actual or anticipated failure of a contractor to fulfill the terms and conditions of the contract, thus giving the contracting officer the right to terminate the contract. [NCMA-SC] (2) The failure to perform a legal obligation or duty. [FBL]

DEFAULT TERMINATION Sanction that the government may impose, under the standard Default clause, for a contractor's failure to perform. [GUIDE] See also "Cure Notice"; "Show Cause Letter"; and "Termination."

DEFECT The absence of something necessary for completeness or perfection; a deficiency in something essential to the proper use for the purpose for which a thing is to be used. Some structural weakness in part or component that is responsible for damage. [BLD2]

DEFECT, LATENT Defects that existed at the time of acceptance but would not have been discovered by a reasonable inspection. [NC-A]

DEFECT, PATENT Defects that can be discovered without undue effort. If the defects were actually known to the government [buyer] at the time of acceptance they are patent, even if they might otherwise not have been discoverable by a reasonable inspection. [NC-A]

DEFECTIVE COST OR PRICING DATA Certified cost or pricing data subsequently found to have been inaccurate, incomplete, or nonconcurrent as of the effective date of the certificate. [OPM]

DEFECTIVE PRICING ACTION If after contract award, cost or pricing data relied upon by the PCO are found to be inaccurate, incomplete, or noncurrent as of the date of final agreement on price given on the contractor's or subcontractor's Certificate of Current Cost or Pricing Data, the government is entitled to a price adjustment, including profit or fee, of any amount by which the price was increased because of the defective data. [Navy]

DEFECTIVE SPECIFICATIONS Mistakes and omissions in the requirements set forth are generally identified in this way. This area is frequently the basis for claims and litigation between contracting parties. [Cohen]

DEFENSE ACQUISITION CIRCULAR (DAC) Circular that is issued to revise or supplement the Department of Defense Supplement to the Federal Acquisition Regulation (Defense Federal Acquisition Regulation Supplement, or DFARS). [GUIDE]

DEFENSE ACQUISITION REGULATION (DAR) The regulation that governed Department of Defense procurements directly before the Federal Acquisition Regulation became effective in 1984. [McVay]

DEFENSE ACQUISITION REGULATORY COUNCIL (DARC) A council comprised of representatives of the secretary of Defense, the Army, the Navy, the Air Force, the Defense Logistics Agency, and NASA. Among other responsibilities, this Council, along with the Civilian Acquisition Council (CAAC), maintains the FAR. [FAI]

DEFENSE CONTRACT AUDIT AGENCY (DCAA) Separate and independent entity within the Defense Department that provides contract audit functions and accounting-financial advisory services for all Defense Department components, as well as for other government agencies. [GUIDE]

DEFENSE FEDERAL ACQUISITION REGULATION SUPPLEMENT (DFARS) Establishes for the Defense Department uniform policies and procedures that implement the Federal Acquisition Regulation (FAR), as well as supplementary material that is unique to DOD. The DFARS is not a stand-alone document and must be read in conjunction with the FAR. [Navy]

DEFENSE LOGISTICS AGENCY (DLA) Component organization within the Defense Department that provides consumable supply items and logistics services common to the military services. [GUIDE]

DEFENSE PRIORITIES AND ALLOCATIONS SYSTEM (DPAS) A set of laws and regulations that establishes priorities for all contracts and subcontracts issued (1) for domestic and imported steel, copper, aluminum, or nickel alloys; and (2) for performance of any of forty defense-related programs. [McVay] See also "Priority Ratings."

DEFERRED PROCUREMENT A decision that the initial procurement quantity of high cost items is to be less than the originally estimated quantity during a specified support period. [OPM]

DEFICIT A deficit occurs when more is spent than is received in a fiscal year.

It grows as one year's overspending is added to next year's. [DLA]

DEFINITE-QUANTITY CONTRACT A contractual instrument that provides for a definite quantity of supplies or services to be delivered at some later, unspecified date. [McVay]

DEFLATED HOURLY RATES See "Uncompensated Overtime."

DELAY, EXCUSABLE (1) A contractual provision designed to protect the contractor from sanctions for late performance. To the extent that it has been excusably delayed, the contractor is protected from default termination, liquidated damages, or excess costs of reprocurement or completion. Excusable delays also may lead to recovery of additional compensation if the government constructively accelerates performance. [NC-A]
(2) Excusable delay protects contractors from penalties for delays that are beyond their control. Examples of excusable delay are acts of God or the public enemy, acts of the government in either its sovereign or contractual capacity, fire, flood, quarantines, strikes, epidemics, unusually severe weather, and freight embargoes. [FAR]

DELAY, GOVERNMENT-CAUSED Acts of the government in either its sovereign or contractual capacity may be found to be excusable causes of delay. For a contractor to be excused by an act of the government in its contractual capacity, the contractor must prove that the government act causing the delay was wrongful. Sovereign acts that delay the contractor's performance are grounds for excusable delays. [NC-A]

DELEGATION The conferring of authority, from one government agency or representative to another, to accomplish contract administrative tasks. Such authority may be shared or recalled. [L&P II]

DELEGATION OF PROCUREMENT AUTHORITY (DPA) An act whereby authority to procure supplies and services is transmitted to another. For example, the General Services Administration (GSA) delegates authority to agencies or activities to procure Automatic Data Processing Equipment. [FIRMR]

DELINQUENCY The actual or potential failure by the contractor to meet or maintain the contract delivery or performance schedule. [AFIT]

DELIVERY (1) Transfer of possession. A "Delivery Order" directs an established source to transfer possession of goods from the source to the ordering activity. Applied to shipping, delivery occurs when a bill of lading is surrendered and title of goods passes to the receiver or consignee. [FAI II]
(2) Constructive or actual delivery; the performance of services for the customer or requisitioner; accessorial services, when they are normally recorded in the billing and collection cycle immediately following performance. [MSA]

DELIVERY ORDER A written order to a contractor pursuant to an indefinite-delivery type contract, which then becomes the basic obligating document for the transaction. Consummation of an originally partial contractual agreement between the contractor and the government. [OPM]
See also "Indefinite-Delivery/Indefinite-Quantity Contract."

DEPOSITION Testimony that is taken under oath and subject to cross-examination in order to discover what the witness is going to say and to ensure the preservation of the witness's testimony should the witness die or disappear or forget before the trial. [FBL]

DESCRIPTIVE LITERATURE Information, such as cuts, illustrations, drawings, and brochures, that shows the characteristics or construction of a product or explains its operation. [FAR]

DESIGN CRITERIA Design constraints or preferred or accepted techniques to be used in achieving an acceptable approach to a design requirement. [AFIT]

DESIGN SPECIFICATION (1) A document (including drawings) setting forth the required characteristics of a particular component, part, subsystem, system, or construction item. [L&P II]
(2) A purchase description that establishes precise measurements, tolerances, materials, in-process and finished product tests, quality control, inspection requirements, and other specific details of the deliverable. [FAI]

DESIGN-TO-COST A concept that establishes cost elements as management goals to achieve the best balance between life cycle cost, acceptable performance, and schedule. Under this concept, cost is a design constraint during the design and development phases and a management discipline throughout the acquisition and operation of the system or equipment. [FAR]

DESK AUDIT An examination of limited scope made at a point removed from the site of operations by means of reference to documents and other available information. [AFIT]

DETERMINATION AND FINDINGS A document signed by an authorized government official justifying a decision to take a certain action; expressed in terms of meeting the regulatory requirements of the situation. [OPM]

DETERMINATION OF RESPONSIBILITY The process by which a contractor is determined to be a responsible bidder/offeror. [OPM]
See also "Responsible Contractor."

DIFFERING SITE CONDITIONS A provision in construction contracts that provides for adjustment of the contract price should the contractor discover physical conditions of an unusual nature that differ from those ordinarily encountered. [McVay]

DIFFERING SITE CONDITIONS— CATEGORY I A subsurface or latent physical condition differing materially from conditions that are indicated in the contract documents or may be implied from other language in the contract documents. [NC-A]

DIFFERING SITE CONDITIONS— CATEGORY II Conditions that are unknown and unusual, differing materially from those ordinarily encountered and not generally recognized as inherent in such work. [NC-A]

DIRECT ALLOCATION OF SALARY COSTS See "Uncompensated Overtime."

DIRECT COST Costs specifically identifiable with a contract requirement, including but not restricted to costs of material and/or labor directly incorporated into an end item. [L&P]

DIRECT COSTING Type of product costing that charges fixed manufacturing overhead immediately against the revenue of the period in which it was incurred, without assigning it to specific units produced. [NCMA-CA]
Also known as "Marginal Costing" and "Variable Costing."

DIRECT LABOR All labor that is obviously related and specifically and conveniently traceable to specific products. [NCMA-CA]

DIRECT MATERIAL Material, including raw material, purchased parts, and subcontracted items, directly incorporated into an end item, which is identifiable to a contract requirement. [L&P]

DIRECT PROCUREMENT The procurement of defense supplies in the United States by a foreign government, contractor, or organization in which the supplies are purchased through commercial channels for use outside of the United States. [AFIT]

DISCHARGE OF A CONTRACT Results when the obligations incurred by the parties when they entered into the agreement are excused, and the parties are no longer bound to perform as promised. [FAI]

DISCLOSURE STATEMENT An official statement in which persons or firms are required to describe their contract cost accounting practices by providing data responsive to the requirements of the government's Cost Accounting Standards. [OPM]

DISCOUNT See "Prompt Payment Discount"; "Quantity Discount"; and "Trade Discount."

DISCOUNTED HOURLY RATES See "Uncompensated Overtime."

DISCOVERY Pretrial or prehearing procedure designed to promote full disclosure of all relevant facts related to a contract dispute. [GUIDE]

DISCUSSION Any oral or written communication between the government and an offeror, other than communications conducted for the purpose of minor clarification, whether or not initiated by the government, that (a) involves information essential for determining the acceptability of a proposal, or (b) provides the offeror an opportunity to revise or modify its proposal. [FAR]

DISPUTES CLAUSE A contract provision providing for administrative consideration and relief for disputes concerning questions of fact under a government contract that cannot be resolved by agreement between the parties to the contract. [OPM]

DOCUMENTATION Recorded technical data, or a concept in any form from which information can be derived. [AFIT]

DOD VOLUNTARY DISCLOSURE PROGRAM See "Voluntary Disclosure Program."

DOMESTIC END PRODUCT Either (a) an unmanufactured end product mined or produced in the United States, or (b) an end product manufactured in the United States, if the cost of its components mined, produced, or manufactured in the United States exceeds 50 percent of the cost of all its components. (In determining if an end product is domestic, only the end product and its components shall be considered.) The cost of each component includes transportation costs to the place of incorporation into the end product and any applicable duty (whether or not a duty-free entry certificate is issued). [FAR] See also "Buy American Act."

DOMESTIC PREFERENCE Any one of a number of policies adopted by a nation's government that maintain discriminatory government procurement rules designed to establish a preference in favor of domestic suppliers. [TIPS(1-15)] See also "Buy American Act."

DRUG-FREE WORKPLACE A site for the performance of work done in connection with a specific contract at which employees of the contractor are prohibited from engaging in the unlawful manufacture, distribution, dispensing, possession, or use of a controlled substance. [FAR]

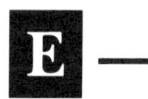

ECONOMIC ORDER QUANTITY (EOQ) This concept holds that the appropriate quantity to order may be the one that tends to minimize all the costs associated with the order—carrying costs, acquisition costs, and the cost of the material itself. The EOQ formula states that EOQ occurs when annual carrying cost = annual acquisition cost (CC = AC). [DBL]

ECONOMIC PRICE ADJUSTMENT An alteration permitted and specified by contract provisions for the upward or downward revision of a stated contract price upon the occurrence of certain specifically defined contingencies. [OPM]

ECONOMICS The study of how people and society choose to employ scarce productive resources to produce goods and services and distribute them among various persons and groups in society. [ECON]

ECONOMY A particular system of organization for the production, distribution, and consumption of all things people use to achieve a certain standard of living. [ECON]

EFFECTIVE COMPETITION A market condition that exists when two or more responsible offerors acting independently contend for a contract that results in the buyer receiving either (1) the lowest cost or price alternative, or (2) the optimal combination of technical design coupled with a cost effective price. [L&P II]

ELASTICITY OF DEMAND Degree of responsiveness of quantity demanded to a change in price. [ECON]

ELECTRONIC DATA INTERCHANGE (EDI) The computer-to-computer exchange of standard business documentation in machine processable form. [EDI]

ELECTRONIC FUNDS TRANSFER (EFT) The company-to-company or company-to-bank electronic exchange of value. [EDI]

ELECTRONIC MAIL (E-Mail) The transfer of messages over computer networks. Messages are usually in free format. [EDI]

ELECTRONIC MAILBOX A designated holding location for electronic messages. The mailbox can either be on the user's computer, or, as is more common, on a third-party network computer. [EDI]

ELECTRONIC PAYMENTS Any method of making payments electronically. Includes wire transfers and Automated Clearing House (ACH) payments. The ACH is an organization that acts as a storage and transfer facility for electronic payments. [EDI]

ELEMENTS OF A CONTRACT Elements that must be present in a contract if the contract is to be binding. These include the following:
* an offer;
* acceptance;
* consideration;
* execution by competent parties;
* legality of purpose; and
* clear terms and conditions. [FAI]

ELEMENTS OF COST Those cost categories that directly or indirectly influence the cost of producing material or providing services and that can be apportioned to the contract. [OPM]

ENCRYPTION A method of ensuring data secrecy. The message to be sent is coded using a key available only to the sender and the receiver. The coded message is sent to the receiver and then decoded upon receipt. [EDI]

END ITEM An assembled whole system or equipment ready for its intended use. [AFIT]

ENGINEERING CHANGE PROPOSAL (ECP) A document proposing any design change requiring revision to contract specifications or engineering drawings; may be originated by either party to a contract; requires detailed documentation and an evaluation of technical, cost, and schedule effects. [OPM]

ENGINEERING DATA Engineering documents such as specifications, drawings, standards, lists, or other information prepared by a design activity relating to the design, performance, manufacture, test, or inspection of items and services. [AFIT]

EQUAL ACCESS TO JUSTICE ACT (EAJA) Federal law designed to aid small businesses and individuals to recover attorney fees if they prevail in certain actions against the government. [GUIDE]

EQUAL EMPLOYMENT OPPORTUNITY (EEO) The right of every individual under the law to be considered for employment without discrimination based on race, color, sex, national origin, age, religion, nondisqualifying mental or physical handicap, or any other nonmerit factor. [Navy]

EQUITABLE ADJUSTMENT The compensation or price adjustment to which a contractor is entitled upon the occurrence of a constructive change or special event. [OPM]

ESCALATION A term traditionally used to indicate an upward or downward movement of price. [OPM]
See also "Economic Price Adjustment."

ESTABLISHED CATALOGUE PRICE A price that is regularly maintained by a manufacturer or vendor, is published or made available for inspection by customers, and which states prices at which sales are currently, or were last, made to a significant number of buyers constituting the general public. [OPM]

ESTABLISHED GOVERNMENT SOURCES Government and nongovernment sources of supplies, equipment, and services that are designated by law or regulation as mandatory sources, in a set order of priority, for particular items and services. [FAI II]

ESTABLISHED MARKET PRICE A current price, established in the usual and ordinary course of trade between buyers and sellers free to bargain, which can be substantiated from sources independent of the manufacturer or vendor. [OPM]

ESTIMATE AT COMPLETION (EAC) Actual direct costs, plus indirect costs allocable to the contract, plus the estimate of costs (direct or indirect) for authorized work remaining. [JIG]

ESTOPPEL A rule of law that bars, prevents, and precludes a party from alleging or denying certain facts because of a previous allegation or denial or because of his or her previous conduct or admission. [FBL]

ETHICS Of or relating to moral action, conduct, motive or character; as, ethical emotion; also, treating of moral feelings, duties or conduct; containing precepts of morality; moral. Professionally right or befitting; conforming to professional standards of conduct. [BLD]

EVALUATION BOARD See "Source Selection Evaluation Board."

EVALUATION FACTORS Factors that will be considered in evaluating proposals tailored to each acquisition that have an impact on the source selection decision. Price or cost to the government shall be included as an evaluation factor in every source selection. Quality shall also be addressed in every source selection. Quality may be expressed in terms of technical excellence, management capability, personnel qualifications, prior experience, past performance, and schedule compliance. Any other relevant factors, such as cost realism, may also be included. [FAR]

EXCESS PERSONAL PROPERTY Property under control of an agency or activity that the agency or activity has declared is excess to its needs. [FAI II]

EXCESS REPROCUREMENT COSTS The contractor is liable to the government for any excess costs incurred by the government to repurchase supplies or services similar to those terminated for default. [FAR]

EXCLUSIVE (NON-EXCLUSIVE) LICENSE A license covering a patent(s), technical or proprietary data, technical assistance, know-how, or any combination of these, granted by a U.S. firm to a foreign firm or government to produce, co-produce, or sell a defense article or service within a given sales territory without competition from any other licensees or from the licensor. A "Non-Exclusive License" is a license as described above, except that competition may be permitted with other licensees and/or the licensor. [MSA]

EXCULPATORY CLAUSES Contract language designed to shift responsibility to the other party. A "no damages for delay" clause would be an example of one used by customers. [Cohen]

EXCUSABLE DELAY See "Delay, Excusable."

EXECUTED CONTRACT A written document, signed by both parties and mailed or otherwise furnished to each party, which expresses the requirements, terms, and conditions to be met by both parties in the performance of the contract. [OPM]

EXPEDITED PROCEDURE Procedure under the Contract Disputes Act whereby an appellant before an agency Board of Contract Appeals can elect, for certain claims, to have a decision issued on a claim within four months after making the election. [GUIDE]
Also known as "Accelerated Procedure."

EXPERT SYSTEMS Computerized knowledge base of basic facts and heuristic (problem-solving) knowledge that assists humans in eliminating infeasible decision options up front. [TIPS(2-8)]

EXPIRED COST A cost that should be released to the current period as an expense or loss. [NCMA-CA]

EXPORT ADMINISTRATION REGULATIONS (EAR) Export of commodities not regulated by the State Department through the International Traffic in Arms Regulation (ITAR) is administered by the Commerce Department through the Export Administration Regulations (EAR). Under the EAR, most commodities can be exported under the authority of a general license. Authority to export commodities that are dual-use items (those that can be used for both defense/spacecraft and commercial purposes) is sought under a validated license. A validated license is necessary to protect national security or foreign policy interests, or because the commodity is in short supply in the United States. [TIPS(2-10)]
See also "International Traffic in Arms Regulation."

EXPRESS Direct, explicit, exact, precise, and specific language that manifests these characteristics and is not left to interpretation or inference. [L&P]

EXPRESS AUTHORITY See "Agent Authority."

EXTENDED WORK WEEK See "Uncompensated Overtime."

EXTRAORDINARY CONTRACTUAL RELIEF Form of relief for contractors under federal law giving the president the power to authorize federal agencies to enter into contracts, or amendments or modifications of contracts, without regard to other provisions of law relating to the making, performance, amendment, or modification of contracts, when the president believes the action will facilitate national defense. [GUIDE]

FACILITIES CAPITAL The net book value of tangible capital assets and of those intangible capital assets that are subject to amortization. [FAR]

FACILITIES CAPITAL COST OF MONEY (FCCM) An imputed cost of capital committed to facilities determined by applying a cost-of-money rate determined by the Secretary of the Treasury to facilities capital employed in contract performance. [FAR]

FACTFINDING The process of identifying and obtaining information necessary to complete the evaluation of proposals. This may include factfinding sessions with offerors. [FAI]

FACTORY BURDEN See "Factory Overhead."

FACTORY OVERHEAD All factory costs other than direct labor and direct material. [NCMA-CA]

Also known as "Factory Burden"; "Indirect Manufacturing Costs"; and "Manufacturing Overhead."

FAIR AND REASONABLE A subjective evaluation of what each party deems as equitable consideration in areas such as terms and conditions, cost or price, assured quality, and timeliness of contract performance, and/or any other areas subject to negotiation. [L&P II]

FAIR AND REASONABLE PRICE A price that is fair to both parties, considering the agreed-upon conditions, promised quality, and timeliness of contract performance. Although generally a fair and reasonable price is a function of the law of supply and demand, there are statutory, regulatory, and judgmental limits on the concept. [ASPM]

FAIR LABOR STANDARDS ACT Federal Act (1938) that set a minimum standard wage (periodically increased by later statutes) and a maximum work week of forty hours in industries engaged in interstate commerce. The Act also prohibited the labor of children under sixteen years of age in most employments, and under eighteen years of age in dangerous occupations. The Act created the Wage and Hour Division in the Department of Labor. [BLD]

FAST PAYMENT PROCEDURE A procedure utilized with small purchases that provides payment to the contractor immediately upon receipt of its invoice (and before inspection and acceptance has taken place), provided the contractor certifies that the supplies have been delivered to a "Point of First Receipt" (such as a common carrier) and are as ordered. [McVay]

See also "Point of First Receipt."

FAST TRACK PROGRAM An acquisition program in which time constraints require the design, development, production, testing, and support acquisition processes to be compressed or overlapped. [DSMC]

FEDERAL ACQUISITION CIRCULAR (FAC) Document issued by the Defense Acquisition Regulatory Council and the Civilian Agency Acquisition Council to amend the Federal Acquisition Regulation. [GUIDE]

FEDERAL ACQUISITION INSTITUTE (FAI) Within the jurisdiction of OFPP, there are two offices designed to carry out parts of its mission—the Federal Acquisition Institute (FAI) and the Federal Procurement Data Center (FPDC). Both have been established under administrative jurisdiction of the General Services Administration. FAI's job is to improve the professional standing of the federal procurement work force. [Sherman2]

Previously known as the "Federal Procurement Institute" (FPI).

FEDERAL ACQUISITION REGULATION (FAR) The government-wide procurement regulation mandated by Congress and issued by the Department of Defense, the General Services Administration, and the National Aeronautics and Space Administration. Effective April 1, 1984, the FAR supersedes both the Defense Acquisition Regulation (DAR) and the Federal Procurement Regulation (FPR). All federal agencies are authorized to issue regulations implementing the FAR. [NCMA-SB]

FEDERAL ACQUISITION REGULATORY COUNCIL A council comprised of the Administrator for the Office of Federal Procurement Policy (OFPP), the Secretary of Defense, the Administrator of National Aeronautics and Space Administration (NASA), and the Administrator of the General Services Administration (GSA). Under the Office of Federal Procurement Policy Act, the Council assists in the direction and coordination of government-wide procurement and policy procurement regulatory activities. [FAI]

FEDERAL ASSISTANCE (GRANTS AND COOPERATIVE AGREEMENTS) (1) The furnishing of assistance (anything of value) by the federal government by grant or cooperative agreement to a recipient to accomplish a public purpose. Different from procurement in that it is not an acquisition of products or services for the direct benefit or use of the federal government. [OPM]
(2) Refers to federal financing for public purposes through transfer of funds to state or local governments or to other recipients. The principal distinction between an assistance arrangement and procurement is found in the purpose of the funding. If the purpose is to sponsor property or to support services not for the government's express use or benefit, assistance arrangements are used. Within the category of assistance, there are two principal types of instruments: the grant and the cooperative agreement. The distinction between the grant and the cooperative agreement relates to management: grants have little or no federal involvement in management, whereas cooperative agreements involve collaborative management from the sponsoring agency. [Sherman3]
See also "Cooperative Agreement" and "Grant."
FEDERAL COURTS IMPROVEMENT ACT Federal law that, in 1982, replaced the U.S. Court of Claims as the primary federal court involved in government contract litigation with two new courts—the U.S. Claims Court and the U.S. Court of Appeals for the Federal Circuit. [GUIDE]
FEDERAL DATA PROCESSING CENTERS (FDPC) Government-managed data processing facilities providing computing services to federal agencies on a cost reimbursable basis. [FIRMR]
FEDERAL INFORMATION RESOURCES MANAGEMENT REGULATION (FIRMR) Codifies uniform policies and procedures pertaining to information resources activities by federal or executive agencies, and by government contractors (FIRMR 210-1.101). The FIRMR is prescribed by the administrator of General Services regarding automatic data processing resources acquisition and management. [FIRMR]
FEDERAL PROCUREMENT DATA CENTER (FPDC) The FPDC is charged with developing and implementing a government-wide procurement data system capable of generating consistent and accurate statistical reports of government-wide procurement activity. [Sherman2]
See also "Federal Acquisition Institute."
FEDERAL PROCUREMENT INSTITUTE (FPI) See "Federal Acquisition Institute."
FEDERAL PROCUREMENT REGULATIONS (FPR) (1) The rules that governed the purchases made by civilian agencies before the Federal Acquisition Regulation became effective. [McVay]
(2) The Federal Procurement Regulations were issued in 1959 to provide detailed procurement guidance and requirements for the non-military agencies. The lead agency for the FPR was the General Services Administration (GSA). The FPR was authorized by the Federal Property and Administrative Services Act of 1949. [Culver]
FEDERAL PROPERTY AND ADMINISTRATIVE SERVICES ACT General federal statute that governs contracting by the civilian agencies of the government. [GUIDE]
FEDERAL REGISTER A daily government publication that informs the public of proposed rules, final rules, and other legal notices issued by federal agencies. [FAI]
FEDERAL SPECIFICATION OR STANDARD A specification or standard issued or controlled by the General Services Administration (GSA) and listed in the GSA Index of Federal Specifications, Standards, and Commercial Item Descriptions. [FAR]
FEDERAL SUPPLY SCHEDULE PROGRAM Directed and managed by the General Services Administration, provides federal agencies with a simplified process for obtaining commonly used supplies and services at prices associated with volume buying. There are four types of Federal Supply Schedules: Single-award, Multiple-award, New Item Introductory, and International. [FAR]

FEE An agreed to amount of reimbursement beyond the initial estimate of costs. [OPM]

The term "Fee" is used when discussing cost-reimbursement contracts, whereas "Profit" is used in relation to fixed-price contracts.

FIDUCIARY A person who handles another person's money or property in a capacity that involves a confidence or trust. Examples of fiduciaries are executors or guardians of the estates of minors or deceased persons. [FBL]

FIELD CONTRACTING ACTIVITY A level of government contracting activity that supports the operational requirements of a post, camp, station, national park, hospital, institute, or field installation, and involves a highly diversified range of assignments. [OPM]

FIELD PRICING SUPPORT The analysis of contractor pricing proposals by any or all field technical and other specialists. [OPM]

FINAL COST OBJECTIVE A cost objective that has allocated to it both direct and indirect costs and, in the contractor's accumulation system, is one of the final accumulation points. [FAR]

FINAL DECISION For purposes of the Contract Disputes Act, a contracting officer's unilateral adjudication of a contract claim that is a prerequisite to jurisdiction over the claim by a Board of Contract Appeals or Federal Court. [GUIDE]

FINANCIAL ACCOUNTING Involves the measuring and recording of financial data of an enterprise for purposes of providing relevant financial information to interested users both internal and external to the entity. [NCMA-CA]

FINANCIAL ACCOUNTING DATA SHEET Commits the government to availability of funds for specific amounts as displayed on the data sheet. It is the final proof the contracting officer needs to show that funds are available to obligate the government. The data sheet becomes the last page of any contract or modification involving money. The data sheet is part of the contract, as opposed to the FAD sheet, which is attached to the Procurement Request (PR) and indicates funding availability. [Navy]

Also known as "Data Sheet."

FINANCIAL ACCOUNTING STANDARDS BOARD (FASB) A professional board created by the American Institute of Certified Public Accountants. Previously named the Accounting Principles Board (APB), the APB was replaced in 1973 by the FASB. The FASB was considered an improvement over the APB, as the FAS Board was more autonomous and carried a broader representation of accountants than the APB. FASB publishes its pronouncements in its Statement of Financial Accounting Standards. FASB also publishes Statements of Financial Accounting Concepts, which set forth fundamental objectives and concepts on which further FASB pronouncements will be based. [NCMA-CA]

FINANCIAL DATA ADDENDUM SHEET A document that indicates funds are available for a particular procurement. It indicates the appropriate funding citation and dollar limitation that is established for procuring the designated item. It is attached to the Procurement Request (PR) or forwarded by separate funding procurement request to initiate the funding action. The FAD sheet is distinguished from the data sheet, which becomes part of the executed contract. [Navy]

Also known as "FAD Sheet."

FINANCING See "Contractor Financing."

FINISHED GOODS INVENTORY The cost of a manufacturer's completed product that is being held for sale. [NCMA-CA]

FIRM BID RULE A rule that prohibits the bidder from withdrawing its bid for the period specified in the Invitation for Bids (IFBs), usually sixty days after bid opening. [McVay]

FIRM-FIXED-PRICE (FFP) CONTRACT A contract that provides for a price that is not subject to any adjustment by reason of costs experienced by the contractor in the performance of the contract. [OPM]

FIRST ARTICLE Preproduction models, initial production samples, test samples, first lots, or pilot samples submitted for testing and evaluation for conformance with specified contract requirements before or in the initial stages of production. [AFIT]

FIRST-IN, FIRST-OUT (FIFO) An inventory costing method where the stock of merchandise or material that is acquired earliest is assumed to be used first; the stock acquired latest is assumed to be still on hand. [MGMT]

FISCAL YEAR (FY) The federal budget cycle, which runs from October 1 to September 30, is known as the government's fiscal year. [DLA]

FISHBONE DIAGRAM Another name for the cause-and-effect diagram. (The finished product resembles a fish skeleton.) Also known as "Ishikawa Diagram" after the Japanese engineer who developed it. [BOE II]
See also "Cause and Effect Diagram."

FITNESS FOR USE The condition of goods and services that meet the needs of people who use them. [BOE II]

FIXED COST A cost which, for a given period of time and range of activity, called the "relevant range," does not change in total but becomes progressively smaller on a per-unit basis as volume increases. [NCMA-CA]

FIXED PRICE A form of pricing that includes a ceiling beyond which the government [buyer] bears no responsibility for payment. [OPM]

FIXED-PRICE-INCENTIVE (FPI) CONTRACT A type of contract that provides for adjusting profit and establishing the final contract price by application of a formula based on the relationship of total final negotiated cost to total target cost. The final price is subject to a price ceiling, negotiated at the outset. There are two types of FPI contracts: firm target and successive targets. [Navy]

FIXED-PRICE REDETERMINABLE (FPR) CONTRACT A fixed-price type of contract that contains provisions for subsequently negotiated adjustment, in whole or in part, of the initially negotiated base price. [OPM]

FIXED-PRICE WITH ECONOMIC PRICE ADJUSTMENT CONTRACT A fixed-price contract that permits an element of cost to fluctuate to reflect current market prices. [McVay]

FLEXIBLE BUDGET A budget, usually referring to overhead costs only, which is prepared for a range, rather than a single level of activity; one which can be automatically geared to changes in the level of volume. [NCMA-CA]
Also known as a "Variable Budget."

FLOW CHART A chart that symbolically shows the input from suppliers, the sequential work activities, and the output to the customer. [BOE II]

FLOW DOWN The transfer and translation of prime contract requirements to subcontracts. [NCMA-SC]

FORCE MAJEURE CLAUSE (1) Excusable conditions for nonperformance, e.g., strikes and acts of God, are contained in this clause. [Cohen]
(2) A French term that refers to an unexpected or uncontrollable event that upsets the plan or releases one from obligation; literally, it means "superior force." [TIPS(2-10)]

FOREIGN CORRUPT PRACTICES ACT In 1977, the Congress passed legislation making certain payments to foreign government officials illegal, even if such payments are legal or a common practice in the foreign country. [TIPS(2-10)]

FOREIGN MILITARY SALES (FMS) (1) Actions on the part of the Department of Defense on behalf of another government to make procurements using that government's funds. [OPM]
(2) That portion of U.S. security assistance authorized by the Foreign Assistance Act of 1961, as amended, and the Arms Export Control Act, as amended, where the recipient provides reimbursement for defense articles and services transferred. FMS includes DOD cash sales from stocks (inventories, services, training); DOD guarantees covering financing by private or Federal Financing Bank sources for credit sales of defense articles and defense services; sales financed by appropriated direct credits; and sales funded by grants under the Military Assistance Program. [MSA]

FORM, FIT, and FUNCTION DATA A type of data that provides a basic technical description of an item's characteristics and capabilities. Its primary purpose is to describe an item to such a degree as to allow the government to procure comparable items. The government generally requires unlimited rights to all form, fit, and function data. [TIPS(2-5)]
See also "Rights in Technical Data."

FORMAL ADVERTISING A method of procurement in which award is made, after an invitation for bids, to the responsible bidder whose bid will be most advantageous to the government. Used for the procurement of well-defined items (Conventional Formal Advertising), or items requiring the submission of technical proposals prior to the submission of prices (Two-Step Formal Advertising). [OPM] This term has been replaced in the FAR by the term "Sealed Bid."

FORWARD BUYING The practice of buying materials in a quantity exceeding specified current requirements, but not beyond the actual foreseeable requirements. Even though not known with precision, it is reasonably certain that a longer-term production need for the material does exist. Any purchases beyond this point fall into the speculative buying category. Forward buying can be used in stable markets or in unstable markets where prices appear to be rising. One potential hazard in forward buying, however, is the possible price risk involved, depending on the volatility of the market in which the purchase is made. The buyer must also consider the additional inventory carrying costs and the attendant tie-up of working capital that accompany forward buys. [DBL]

FORWARD PRICING Action involving negotiations and a resultant agreement between a contractor and the buyer to use certain rates and/or indices for a specified future period of time in pricing contracts or contract modifications. [L&P II]

FRAUD An intentional perversion of truth for the purpose of inducing another in reliance upon it to part with something of value belonging to him or her or to surrender a legal right. A false representation of a matter of fact, whether by words or conduct, by false or misleading allegations, or by concealment of that which should have been disclosed, which deceives and is intended to deceive another so that he or she shall act upon it to his or her legal injury. Anything calculated to deceive. [BLD2]

FREE ON BOARD (FOB) This term is used in conjunction with a physical point to determine (a) the responsibility and basis for payment of freight charges, and (b) unless otherwise agreed, the point at which title for goods passes to the buyer or consignee. *FOB origin*—The seller places the goods on the conveyance by which they are to be transported. Cost of shipping and risk of loss are borne by the buyer. *FOB destination*—The seller delivers the goods on the seller's conveyance at destination. Cost of shipping and risk of loss are borne by the seller. [FAR]

FREEDOM OF INFORMATION ACT (FOIA) (1) Provides that information is to be made available to the public either by (a) publishing it in the Federal Register; (b) providing an opportunity to read and copy records at convenient locations; or (c) upon request, providing a copy of a reasonably described record. [FAR]
(2) The Freedom of Information Act, 5 U.S.C. § 552, enacted in 1966, requires disclosure of government records to any person except as stated in specific exceptions. [TIPS(1-12)]

FRINGE BENEFITS Allowances and services provided to employees in addition to their salaries and wages. Fringe benefits may include, but are not limited to, vacations, sick leave, holidays, military leave, insurance, and supplemental unemployment benefits. [BP(90-11)]

FULL AND OPEN COMPETITION All responsible sources are permitted to compete. [FAR]

FULL DISCLOSURE An accounting principle that states the accountant should adequately disclose all relevant information to facilitate a clear understanding of the preparation of financial statements and to avoid erroneous implications. [NCMA-CA]

FULL SCALE DEVELOPMENT (FSD) PHASE The period when the system/equipment and the principal items necessary for its support are designed, fabricated, tested, and evaluated. The intended output is, as a minimum, a preproduction system that closely approximates the final product, the documentation necessary to enter the production phase, and the test results that demonstrate that the production product will meet stated requirements. [DOD-MMH]

FULL-TIME ACCOUNTING See "Uncompensated Overtime."

FUNCTIONAL SPECIFICATION A purchase description that describes the deliverable in terms of performance characteristics and intended use, including those characteristics that at minimum are necessary to satisfy the intended use. [FAI]

GENERAL ACCOUNTING OFFICE (GAO) Government agency, headed by the Comptroller General of the United States, that is charged by law to settle and adjust claims by and against the government, and which, in the government contract area, renders advance opinions for government disbursement officers, audits their accounts, and decides the merits of protests regarding contract awards. [GUIDE]

GENERAL AND ADMINISTRATIVE (G&A) (1) Indirect expenses related to the overall business. Expenses for a company's general and executive offices, executive compensation, staff services, and other miscellaneous support purposes. [OPM]

(2) Any indirect management, financial, or other expense that
- is not assignable to a program's direct overhead charges for engineering manufacturing, material, etc.; but
- is routinely incurred by or allotted to a business unit; and
- is for the general management and administration of the business as a whole. [L&P]

GENERAL PROVISIONS A collection of contract clauses that are not specific to a given procurement, but are part of a common contract language. [OPM]

GENERAL SERVICES BOARD OF CONTRACT APPEALS (GSBCA) A board that, among other responsibilities, has statutory authority to hear protests related to the acquisition of automatic data processing equipment (ADPE) or related resources. [FAI]

GENERALLY ACCEPTED ACCOUNTING PRINCIPLES (GAAP) A technical term encompassing conventions, rules, and procedures of accounting that are "generally accepted" and have "substantial authoritative support." The GAAP have been developed by agreement on the basis of experience, reason, custom, usage, and to a certain extent, practical necessity, rather than being derived from a formal set of theories. [NCMA-CA]

GOALS OF THE ACQUISITION PROCESS Among the goals of the acquisition process are quality, cost, timeliness, risk, competition, integrity, and socioeconomic objectives. [FAI]

"GOING CONCERN" CONCEPT An accounting concept that assumes the economic entity will last indefinitely (without evidence to the contrary). This concept is critical in order to support and justify important accounting concepts such as depreciation of property, amortization of assets, and other considerations. [NCMA-CA]

GOVERNMENT-CAUSED DELAY See "Delay, Government-Caused."

GOVERNMENT CONTRACTOR DEFENSE (1) Allows a government contractor to escape liability from state law claims brought by injured persons when those claims arise from a contractor's compliance with federal government specifications. [BP(89-13)]

(2) The U.S. Supreme Court explained the government contractor defense in *Boyle v. United Technologies Corp*. Thus, the government contractor defense is also known as the "Boyle Rule." The following steps must be used to apply the Boyle Rule: (1) there must be a uniquely federal interest that conflicts with state law; (2) the government must approve precise contract specifications; (3) the contractor must conform to specifications; and (4) the contractor must warn the government of potential dangers. [TIPS(1-9)]

GOVERNMENT-FURNISHED PROPERTY (GFP) Property in the possession of or acquired by the government and subsequently delivered or otherwise made available to the contractor. [AFIT]

GOVERNMENT-OWNED, CONTRACTOR-OPERATED (GOCO) A facility owned by the government but provided to a contractor for operation to produce goods for the government's use. [OPM]

GOVERNMENT PURPOSE LICENSE RIGHTS (GPLR) A type of data rights unique to the Defense Federal Acquisition Regulation Supplement (DFARS) that is designed as a compromise between the polar rights offered by the "unlimited rights" and "limited rights" categories. GPLR allow the government to use the data for "governmental purposes," including reprocurement purposes, while the contractor retains exclusive commercial rights. The DFARS provides that GPLR generally revert to unlimited rights after no more than five years; however, time limits may be negotiated or extended. [TIPS(2-5)] See also "Rights in Technical Data."

GOVERNMENTAL ACCOUNTING Similar to financial accounting, which involves the measuring and recording of financial data of governmental units to interested users; however, governmental accounting utilizes accounting conventions that are different than those applied to financial accounting. [NCMA-CA]

GRACE COMMISSION A commission of volunteer businessmen and labor leaders appointed by the president in 1982 with a mission to investigate the entire federal bureaucracy and seek out every possible savings opportunity. In its final report on January 16, 1985, the Commission made 2,478 specific recommendations that it estimated would save $424 billion over the next three years. Many recommendations dealt with government acquisition of services and supplies, including major systems and spare parts. [Culver]

GRAMM-RUDMAN-HOLLINGS BALANCED BUDGET AND EMERGENCY DEFICIT CONTROL ACT A 1985 law that provided that the federal budget should be balanced by fiscal year 1991. Per the Act, if Congress does not meet the prescribed deficit target in any year, the law requires automatic, across-the-board spending cuts divided evenly between defense and domestic spending. [TIPS(1-5)]

GRANTS (1) Contribution, gift, or subsidy made by the government for specified purposes. Grant is frequently made conditional upon an action specified by the grantee, such as the maintenance of certain standards or a proportional contribution of funds. [AFIT]

(2) Under a grant arrangement, there is little or no federal involvement in the management of the work being funded. Substantial funding of nonfederal, governmental undertakings is provided by the grant process. In addition, research grants are awarded in substantial number by some government agencies. [Sherman3]

See also "Cooperative Agreement" and "Federal Assistance."

GRATUITY Something of monetary value, freely given to someone else with no explicit expectation of return or reward. In actual practice, the motive behind dispensing a gratuity is often suspect, as if the giver were bribing or buying special consideration. [FAI II]

GREEN TIME See "Uncompensated Overtime."

GROSS NATIONAL PRODUCT (GNP) The total dollar value of all the final goods (as distinguished from goods still in the process of production) produced by all the firms in the economy. [ECON]

GUARANTEED LOANS (1) An extraordinary method of contract financing in which the government guarantees payment to the lending institution should the contractor be unable to pay. [McVay]

(2) Guarantees made by federal reserve banks, on behalf of designated guaranteeing agencies, to enable a contractor to obtain financing from private sources under contracts for the acquisition of supplies or services for the national defense. [FAI]

H,I,J

HARD SAVINGS Cost reductions that are reasonable, measurable, and which reduce the established level of approved expenditures. [AFIT]

HISTORICAL COSTS An accounting convention that is the foundation for the valuation of assets and the initial recording of economic transactions. There are various other costing methods that have evolved over time (e.g., present value of future cash flow, etc.), but the historical costs method has been generally accepted by accountants to be the most useful and reliable basis for accounting because (1) historical costs are definite and determinable; and (2) historical costs are objective and verifiable. [NCMA-CA] Also known as "Sunk Costs."

IDLE TIME A time interval during which either the workman, the equipment, or both do not perform useful work. [DOD-MMH]

IMMATERIALITY See "Materiality and Immateriality."

IMPLIED AUTHORITY See "Agent Authority."

IMPLY To indirectly convey meaning or intent; to leave the determination of meaning up to the receiver of the communication based upon circumstances, general language used, or conduct of those involved. [L&P]

IMPREST FUND A cash fund of a fixed amount established by advance of funds, without charge to an appropriation, from an agency finance or disbursing officer to a duly appointed cashier, for disbursement as needed from time to time in making payment in cash for relatively small purchases. [FAR]

IMPROVEMENT CURVE See "Learning Curve."

IN SCOPE Phrase used to denote that an action performed or requested to be performed by a contractor for the buyer could reasonably be considered to be within the requirements of the contract. [L&P II]

INCENTIVE ARRANGEMENT A negotiated pricing arrangement that structures a series of relationships designed to motivate and reward the contractor for performance in accordance with the contract specifications; involves target costs, fees, and/or profits; in the case of award fee arrangements, it involves the payment of a fee tied to negotiated incentive criteria. [OPM]

INCIDENTALS Small items and expenses. In small purchases procurement, incidentals are usually taken care of from the imprest fund. [FAI II]

INCREMENTAL BUDGET The budget is based on the previous period's budget and actual results. The budget amount is then changed in accordance with expectations for the next period. [MGMT]

INCREMENTAL COST Defined narrowly, "Incremental Cost" is the additional cost associated with increases in a given set of costs. For example, the incremental costs of increasing production for 1,000 units to 1,200 per week would be the additional costs of the extra 200 units. Defined broadly, "incremental" is a synonym for "differential"; that is, an incremental may be a positive or negative amount. [MGMT]

INDEFINITE-DELIVERY/ INDEFINITE-QUANTITY (IDIQ) CONTRACT A type of contract in which the exact date of delivery or the exact quantity, or a combination of both, is not specified at the time the contract is executed; provisions are placed in the contract to later stipulate these elements of the contract. [OPM] See also "Delivery Order."

INDEMNIFICATION CLAUSE This clause describes protections provided by the parties to each other. [Cohen]

INDEPENDENT RESEARCH AND DEVELOPMENT (IR&D) The cost of effort that is neither sponsored by a grant, nor required in performing a contract, and which falls within any of the following four areas: (a) basic research, (b) applied research, (c) development, and (d) systems and other concept formulation studies. [FAR]

INDEX NUMBERS The Department of Labor's Bureau of Labor Statistics (BLS) offers publications that provide statistical samples that assist the cost estimator. The *Wholesale Prices and Price Indexes* is a monthly report on price movements at the primary market level, including statistical summary tables and indexes for groups of products and commodities. An annual Supplement contains changes in the relative importance of components of the index, revisions in coverage, and annual averages. The *Consumer Price Index Detailed Report* is a monthly report that contains detailed data used to measure retail price changes, the purchasing power of the consumer's dollar, and inflation. [CE]

INDEX OF FEDERAL SPECIFICATIONS, STANDARDS, AND COMMERCIAL ITEM DESCRIPTIONS See "Federal Specification or Standard."

INDICTMENT A formal accusation of a crime by a grand jury. [FBL]

INDIRECT COST Any cost not directly identifiable with a specific cost objective, but subject to two or more cost objectives. [OPM]
INDIRECT LABOR All labor that is not specifically associated with or cannot be practically traced to specific units of output. [NCMA-CA]
INDIRECT MANUFACTURING COSTS See "Factory Overhead."
INDUSTRIAL BASE A nation's resources that represent the nation's capacity and capability to produce goods at an appropriate rate in terms of national defense and commercial competitiveness. The defense industrial base is only one portion of the whole industrial base, i.e., those industries that at any particular time support the nation's security through the provision of defense material and supporting goods and services. [TIPS(3-2)]
INDUSTRIAL MODERNIZATION INCENTIVES PROGRAM (IMIP) Provides government incentives to contractors to motivate investment of their own funds in facility improvements, which should result in reduced acquisition costs and improved productivity. [DSMC]
INDUSTRY SPECIFICATION Type of specification prepared by technical or industry associations that is approved for use by federal agencies. [GUIDE]
INFLATION An ongoing general rise in prices. The steeper this rise, the faster the decline of a dollar's purchasing power. [ECON]
INITIAL PRODUCT INSPECTION The product verification inspection performed during early stages of production on selected characteristics of an item to obtain confidence that the contractor can produce the item in accordance with contract requirements. [AFIT]
INJUNCTION An order of a court of equity that tells a person to do or refrain from doing some act or acts. [FBL]
INSIDER TRADING Trading in securities, or buying or selling property or assets, on the basis of non-public information acquired during a consultancy contract. [UNI]
INSPECTION The examination (including testing) of supplies and services (including, when appropriate, raw materials, components, and intermediate assemblies) to determine whether the supplies and services conform to the contract requirements. [GSA]
INSPECTION REQUIREMENTS Instructions issued by the purchasing officer or technical representative regarding the type and extent of government inspections required for specific contracts. [AFIT]
INTEGRATED LOGISTICS SUPPORT (ILS) The composite of actions necessary to assure the effective and economical performance of the systems and equipment that, functioning together, comprise a total system and, in turn, an operating force. [Navy]
INTEGRATION, HORIZONTAL A firm that owns several plants, each of which does the same thing, is said to have "Horizontal Integration." An example is retail stores. [ECON]
INTEGRATION, VERTICAL Firms that own several plants, each of which handles a different stage in the production process, are said to have "Vertical Integration." An example of a firm that is vertically integrated is an automobile company that owns iron mines, ore-carrying freighter, steel mills, stamping plants, and assembly plants. [ECON]
INTERDIVISION WORK AUTHORIZATION (IDWA)/INTERDIVISION WORK ORDER (IDWO, IWO) See "Interorganizational Transfer."
INTERNAL CONTROL The coordinated methods and measures in an organization designed to (1) promote efficiency; (2) encourage adherence to prescribed management plans and policies; (3) check the accuracy and validity of organization data; and (4) safeguard assets. [NCMA-CA]
INTERNATIONAL TRAFFIC IN ARMS REGULATION (ITAR) A document prepared by the Office of Munitions Control, Department of State, providing licensing and regulatory provisions for the export of defense articles, technical data, and services. The ITAR also provides the U.S. Munitions List. [MSA]
  See also "Export Administration Regulation."
INTERORGANIZATIONAL TRANSFER (IOT) The assignment of work under a contract to one or more sepa-

rate divisions or subunits of the prime contractor. [NCMA-SC]
Also known as "Interdivision Work Authorization" (IDWA) and "Interdivision Work Order" (IDWO, IWO).

INVENTORIABLE COST A cost associated with units produced; a cost that may be looked upon as "attaching" or "clinging" to units produced. [NCMA-CA]

INVENTORY The amount of property on hand at any given time. [FAI II]

INVESTMENT GOODS See "Capital."

INVITATION FOR BIDS (IFB) The solicitation is called an "Invitation for Bids" when using the sealed-bid method of procurement. [NCMA-SB]
See also "Request for Proposal."

ISHIKAWA DIAGRAM See "Fishbone Diagram."

JACKET Term used to describe the folder in which a procurement request and all associated papers flow through the system. A label is applied to the front of each jacket to identify the Purchase Request (PR) number. The original PR and copies are forwarded in the jacket to the contract specialist. [Navy]

JAVITS-WAGNER-O'DAY (JWOD) ACT Another name for P.L. 92-28, which requires the government to buy some of its supplies and services from nonprofit agencies that employ Americans who are blind or have other severe limitations, such as the Committee for Purchase from the Blind and Other Severely Handicapped (CPBOSH). [NCMA-PSP]

JOB ORDER COST SYSTEM One in which a contractor accounts for output and costs incurred by specifically identifiable physical units. A job order may cover the production of one unit or represent a composite number of identical units. [Cohen]

JOB SHOP A company specializing in the supply of personnel on a temporary basis. [Cohen]

JOINT COST A cost that is common to all the segments in question and that is not clearly or practically allocable except by some questionable allocation base. [NCMA-CA]
Also known as "Common Cost."

JOINT PRODUCTS COSTS Costs of two or more manufactured goods, of significant sales values, that are produced by a single process and that are not identifiable as individual products up to a certain state of production known as the split-off point. [NCMA-CA]

JURISDICTION The authority (of a board of contract appeals, federal court, or arbitrator) to hold a hearing, grant relief, and make determinations that are binding on the parties. [GUIDE]

JUST IN TIME (JIT) INVENTORY (1) A manufacturing and inventory philosophy in which inventory is scheduled for delivery only as needed on the production line. [EDI]
(2) The minimum inventory required to meet production schedules. [BOE II]

JUSTIFICATION AND APPROVAL (J&A) A document to justify procurement using other than full and open competition. This document is required prior to commencing negotiation for a contract resulting from an unsolicited proposal or any other contract award that does not provide for full and open competition. [Navy]

KEY FUNCTIONAL CHARACTERISTICS Those functional qualities or characteristics that critically affect a configuration item's ability to fulfill operational requirements. [AFIT]

KICKBACKS Payment back of a portion of the purchase price to a buyer or public official by the seller to induce purchase or to influence improperly future purchases or leases. A federal statute makes kickbacks a criminal offense in connection with a contract for construction or repair of a public building or a building financed by loans from the government. [BLD]

LABOR HOUR CONTRACT (1) A contract that provides for reimbursement of the contractor's labor costs at a fixed hourly rate. [McVay]
(2) A variation of the time-and-materials contract, differing only in that materials are not supplied by the contractor. [FAI]

LABOR SURPLUS AREA A geographic area identified by the Department of

Labor in accordance with 20 C.F.R. 654, Subpart A, as an area of concentrated unemployment or underemployment or an area of labor surplus. [FAR]

LAST IN, FIRST OUT (LIFO) A cost-flow assumption that the stock acquired earliest is still on hand; the stock of merchandise or material acquired latest is used first. [MGMT]

LAW OF AGENCY See "Agency."

LEARNING CURVE A tool of calculation used primarily to project resource requirements, in terms of direct manufacturing labor hours or the quantity of material (for this purpose, usually referred to as an improvement curve) required for a production run. Used interchangeably with the term "improvement curve," the concept of a learning curve was adopted from the observation that individuals who perform repetitive tasks exhibit a rate of improvement due to increased manual dexterity. [ASPM]

LETTER CONTRACT A written preliminary contractual instrument that authorizes the immediate commencement of activity under its terms and conditions, pending definitization of a fixed-price or cost-reimbursement pricing arrangement for the work to be done. Includes specifications of the government's [buyer's] maximum liability and must be superseded by a definite contract within a specified time. [OPM]

LETTER OF INTENT (LOI) An obligation instrument that can be used to protect price and availability of long-lead time items and for other purposes. [AFIT]

LEVEL OF EFFORT (LOE) The devotion of talent or capability to a predetermined level of activity, over a stated period of time, on the basis of a fixed-price or cost-reimbursement pricing arrangement; payment is usually based on effort expended rather than on results achieved. [OPM]

LEVEL UNIT PRICING The requirement in most multiyear contracts to price each year's deliveries at the same unit price. [McVay]

LICENSE See "Exclusive License."

LIFE CYCLE COST Total cost of an item or system over its entire lifetime, including cost of development, procurement, operation, maintenance, and disposal. [NCMA-SS]

LIMITATION OF COSTS CLAUSE Applicable only to fully funded cost-reimbursement contracts. Under this clause, the contracting officer should be given sixty days notice in writing when costs incurred will exceed 75 percent of the estimated cost. The government is not obligated to reimburse the contractor for costs incurred in excess of the estimated costs, and the contractors are not obligated to continue performance under a contract causing them to incur costs in excess of the estimated costs. [TIPS(1-5)]

See also "Notification Clause."

LIMITATION OF FUNDS CLAUSE Used for incrementally funded cost-reimbursement contracts. Similar to the Limitation of Costs clause, this clause requires the contractor to give the contracting officer sixty days written notice when costs incurred will exceed 75 percent of the funds allotted to the contract. [TIPS(1-5)]

See also "Notification Clause."

LIMITED PRODUCTION See "Low Rate Initial Production."

LIMITED RIGHTS In technical data, refers to the rights to use, duplicate, or disclose technical data in whole or in part, by or for the government, with the express written permission of the party furnishing the technical data. Such data may be released or disclosed outside the government; used by the government for manufacture (or if software documentation, for preparing the same or similar software); or used by a party other than the government except under certain restricted circumstances. [DSMC]

See also "Rights in Technical Data."

LIQUIDATED DAMAGES A contract provision providing for the assessment of damages on the contractor for its failure to comply with certain performance or delivery requirements of the contract; used when the time of delivery or performance is of such importance that the government [buyer] may reasonably expect to suffer damages if the delivery or performance is delinquent. [OPM]

LOAN GUARANTEES See "Guaranteed Loans."

LOCAL BUYING Patronizing local suppliers can have the following benefits: improved community relations; smaller quantities of materials can be provided at lower prices; local inventories can be adapted for continuing local users; minimal transportation costs; and shorter lead times. [DBL]

LOCAL SUPPLIER A business located within the purchasing activity's recognized metropolitan area. [FAI II]

LONG-LEAD ITEMS/LONG-LEAD TIME MATERIALS Components of a system or piece of equipment for which the times to design and fabricate are the longest, and, therefore, to which an early commitment of funds may be desirable in order to meet the earliest possible date of system completion. Might be ordered during "Full Scale Development" (FSD) to arrive for production start. [DSMC]

LOW RATE INITIAL PRODUCTION A low rate of output at the end of Full Scale Development or beginning of production. Reduces the government's [buyer's] exposure to large retrofit problems and costs while still providing adequate numbers of hard tooled production items for final development and operational tests prior to a full production decision. Part of an acquisition strategy, it is a risk reduction method that is also known as "Limited Production" and "Pilot Production." [DSMC]

'M' ACCOUNT Another term for the Treasury Memorandum Account, which was established in 1956 to help lighten the burden of GAO audits and Congress' lengthy appropriations process every year, and to facilitate Congressional appropriations without established ceilings. Individual agency M Accounts were abolished in 1991. [TIPS(2-6)]

MAINTAINABILITY The ability of an item to be retained in or restored to a specified condition when maintenance is performed by personnel having specified skill levels, using prescribed procedures and resources, at each prescribed level of maintenance and repair. [DOD-MMH]

MAJOR SYSTEMS ACQUISITION See "OMB Circular A-109."

MAKE-OR-BUY PROGRAM That part of a contractor's written plan for the development or production of an end item outlining the subsystems, major components, assemblies, subassemblies, and parts intended to be manufactured, test-treated, or assembled by the contractor (make); and those the contractor intends to procure from another source (buy). [DSMC]

MANAGEMENT RESERVE Synonymous with "Management Reserve Budget." An amount of the total allocated budget withheld for management control purposes rather than designated for the accomplishment of a specific task or set of tasks. It is not a part of the Performance Measurement Baseline. [JIG]

MANAGER, KEY FUNCTIONS OF The broad skills or functions of a manager are as follows: planning, organizing, staffing, directing, and controlling. [NCMA-CP2]

MANAGERIAL ACCOUNTING See "Cost Accounting."

MANDATORY FLOW-DOWN CLAUSES Federal Acquisition Regulation (FAR) clauses that are cited in the prime contract and specifically require the inclusion of the text of the clause either verbatim or substantially verbatim in all subcontracts entered into in support of the prime contract. [OPM]

MANDATORY SOURCE See "Established Government Sources."

MANUFACTURING OVERHEAD See "Factory Overhead."

MANUFACTURING RESOURCE PLANNING A production planning and control system used to schedule production jobs, purchase materials, check capacity requirements, forecast product demands, and redirect material supplies in the face of changing schedules. [L&P II]

MANUFACTURING TECHNOLOGY (MANTECH) Any action having the objective of the timely establishment or improvement of the manufacturing process, techniques, or equipment required to support current and projected programs; and the assurance of the availability to produce, reduce lead time, ensure economic availability of end items, reduce costs, increase efficiency, improve reliability, or to enhance safety and anti-pollution measures. [DSMC]

MARCH-IN RIGHTS With respect to any invention of a contractor conceived or first actually reduced to practice in the performance of work under a government contract in which a contractor has acquired title, the agency shall have the right to require the contractor to grant a nonexclusive, partially exclusive, or exclusive license in any field of use to a responsible applicant or applicants. If the contractor refuses such a request, the agency is granted a license if the agency determines that such action is necessary. [FAR]

MARGINAL COSTING See "Direct Costing."

MARKET DIVISION Agreements or understandings by which competitors divide a market in which they compete; exclusive allocation of customers, territories, or products within a market. [BOE]

MARKET RESEARCH The process used for collecting and analyzing information about the entire market available to satisfy the minimum agency needs to arrive at the most suitable approach to acquiring, distributing, and supporting supplies and services. [FAR]

MARKET SURVEY Attempts to ascertain whether other qualified sources capable of satisfying the government's requirement exist. [FAR]

MASTER SOLICITATION A document containing special clauses and provisions that have been identified as essential for the acquisition of a specific type of supply or service that is acquired repetitively. [FAR]

MATCHING PRINCIPLE An important accounting principle that provides the basis for accrual accounting. The matching principle is concerned with matching expenses to the related revenue as a means of providing an accurate presentation of an entity's performance. [NCMA-CA]

See also "Accrual Accounting."

MATERIAL INSPECTION AND RECEIVING REPORT A validated report of contractor-furnished supplies or services inspected and/or accepted by the government. [AFIT]

MATERIAL MANAGEMENT AND ACCOUNTING SYSTEM (MMAS) The contractor's system for planning, controlling, and accounting for the acquisition, use, and disposition of material. Such a system may be manual or automated and may be integrated with planning, engineering, estimating, purchasing, inventory, and/or accounting systems, etc., or may be essentially a stand-alone system. [L&P II]

MATERIAL REQUIREMENTS PLANNING (MRP) A technique used to determine the quantity and timing requirements of "dependent demand" materials used in the manufacturing operation (those materials whose use is directly dependent on the scheduled production of a larger component or finished product). In practice, the actual number-crunching and paperwork generation usually is accomplished by computer, which takes the master production schedule output for a given product and calculates precisely the specific part and component requirements for that product during the given period of operation. [DBL]

MATERIALITY AND IMMATERIALITY An accounting principle that holds that financial reporting is not concerned with insignificant items or minor amounts that would not affect the decisions of interested users. Decisions have to be made regarding the relative importance and size (i.e., materiality) of these expense items in order to determine the most cost-effective and meaningful expression of a company's operating costs. [NCMA-CA]

MATERIALS MANAGEMENT An integrated systems approach to the coordination of materials activities and the control of total materials costs. It advocates assigning to a single operating department all major activities that contribute to the cost of materials. In the classic materials management organization, the following activities report to the materials manager: purchasing; inbound traffic; production scheduling; inventory control; and stores and receiving. [DBL]

MEASURING UNIT In accounting, a standard unit of measure is necessary to provide a "yardstick" for measuring and comparing performance on financial statements. The U.S. dollar is the unit of measure used by virtually all companies in the United States for financial reporting purposes. However, the accounting process assumes that the U.S. dollar remains stable. There are inherent flaws with this assumption (i.e., inflation and deflation of the dollar). [NCMA-CA]

MEMORANDUM OF AGREEMENT (MOA)/ MEMORANDUM OF UNDERSTANDING (MOU) (1) The documentation of mutually agreed to statement of facts, intentions, procedures, and parameters for future actions and matters of coordination. [AFIT]
(2) A "Memorandum of Understanding" may express mutual understanding of an issue without implying commitments by parties to the understanding. [DSMC]

METHOD OF PROCUREMENT The process employed for soliciting offers, evaluating offers, and awarding a contract. In federal contracting, contracting officers use one of the following methods for any given acquisition:
• small purchase;
• sealed bidding;
• negotiation; or
• two-step sealed bidding. [FAI]

MILESTONES Key event points upon which activities are measured for progress. [Cohen]

MILITARY SPECIFICATIONS Specifications and standards maintained by DOD and published in the DOD Index of Specifications and Standards. [FAI]

MILITARY STANDARD REQUISITIONING AND ISSUE PROCEDURES (MILSTRIP) A uniform procedure established by the Department of Defense to govern requisition and issue of material within standardized priorities. [AFIT]

MILLER ACT The Miller Act (40 U.S.C. 270a-270f) requires performance and payment bonds for any construction contract exceeding $25,000, except that this requirement may be waived (1) by the contracting officer for as much of the work as is to be performed in a foreign country upon finding that it is impracticable for the contractor to furnish such bond, or (2) as otherwise authorized by the Miller Act or other law. [FAR]

MISTAKE IN BID A procedure that enables a bidder to correct or withdraw its bid when a mistake has been made in preparing the bid. [McVay]

MODEM Modulator-demodulator. A device that converts information from a computer into an audio tone that can be passed over telephone wires. [EDI]

MODIFICATION See "Contract Modification."

MONOPOLIZATION Maintaining or expanding a large market share through illegal or threatening tactics intended to impair the commercial viability of competitors. [BOE]

MONOPOLY Form of market structure in which the entire market for a good or service is supplied by a single seller or firm. [ECON]

MONOPSONY Market structure in which a single buyer purchases a good or service. [ECON]

MULTIYEAR CONTRACT (1) A method of procuring known requirements for supplies or services for more than one year, even though the total funds obligated are not available at the time of entering into the contract. [OPM]
(2) A fixed-price contract, lasting up to five years, that is funded on a yearly basis with cancellation costs being paid the contractor if the contract is canceled before completion. [McVay]
(3) A procurement of more units of products than can be funded by the government [buyer] in a single year. The total purchase is divided into annual segments that are negotiated at one time. Under multiyear considerations, the government [buyer] pays lower unit prices due to larger buys; however, the contractor is protected from annual cancellations through clauses in the contract. [DOD-MMH]

MUNITIONS LIST The U.S. Munitions List is an enumeration of defense articles and defense services published in the International Traffic in Arms Regulation (ITAR). [MSA]

MUTUAL MISTAKE A mistake is a belief that is not in accord with the facts. If the government participated in the mistake, relief is sought by contractors under the theory of mutual mistake. [NC-A]

— N —

NATIONAL STOCK NUMBER A thirteen-digit number assigned to each part in the government's inventory. [McVay]

NEGOTIATED CEILING Maximum negotiated value for which the government [buyer] is liable for payment to the contractor. [AFIT]
  See also "Adjusted Ceiling."

NEGOTIATED CONTRACT COST The estimated cost negotiated in a cost-plus-fixed-fee contract, or the negotiated contract target cost in either a fixed-price-incentive or cost-plus-incentive-fee contract. [AFIT]

NEGOTIATION (1) A process between buyers and sellers seeking to reach mutual agreement on a matter of common concern through fact-finding, bargaining, and persuasion. [L&P]
  (2) Government acquisition of supplies or services, including construction, by other-than-sealed-bidding procedures. [L&P]

NON-DEVELOPMENTAL ITEM (NDI) A generic term describing either a commercial product or an item developed and used prior to a planned acquisition. Use of a NDI reduces R&D costs and speeds up the acquisition process. [DSMC]
  Also known as an "Off-the-Shelf" item. See also "Commercial Item."

NON-EXCLUSIVE LICENSE See "Exclusive License."

NONPROBABILITY SAMPLING See "Sampling."

NONRECURRING COSTS Costs that are generally incurred on a one-time basis. For example, nonrecurring production costs could include such costs as plant or equipment relocation, plant rearrangement, special tooling and special test equipment, preproduction engineering, initial spoilage and rework, and specialized work force training. [FAR]

NORMAL COSTING A type of product costing that applies to units produced (as costs of production), the actual direct materials consumed, the actual direct labor used, and an estimated, predetermined portion of overhead calculated on the basis of a normal or average schedule of production. [NCMA-CA]

NORMAL WORKWEEK A workweek of forty hours. [FAR]

NOTICE OF AWARD A notification to the lowest, responsive construction contractor that it must obtain a performance bond and a payment bond before it can be awarded a contract. [McVay]

NOTIFICATION CLAUSE For certain types of cost reimbursable contracts, buyers will include provisions that they be notified when invoiced costs reach a percentage of the total contract. This is to allow for proper planning, particularly when it appears that costs identified for the job will not be sufficient to complete the work. [Cohen]
  See also "Limitation of Costs Clause" and "Limitation of Funds Clause."

NOT-TO-EXCEED (NTE) PRICE A maximum price that the contractor may not exceed while negotiations are underway to establish the final price. Permits the contractor to perform the contract while negotiations are being conducted and protects the government [buyer] from excessive expenditures; also a ceiling for a particular cost element in a cost reimbursable contract. [NCMA-SB]

NOVATION AGREEMENT A legal instrument executed by (a) the contractor (transferor), (b) the successor in interest (transferee), and (c) the government [buyer] by which, among other things, the transferor guarantees performance of the contract, the transferee assumes all obligations under the contract, and the government [buyer] recognizes the transfer of the contract and related assets. [FAR]

NO-YEAR FUNDING Congressional funding that does not require obligation in any specific year or years. [FAR]

— O —

OBJECTIVITY An accounting principle that holds that financial accounting information should be verifiable and substantially capable of reproduction for reviews made by independent and qualified preparers utilizing the same set of facts and assumptions. This principle is critical to the audit process. [NCMA-CA]

OBLIGATION A legal requirement for the disbursement of funds based on orders placed, contracts awarded, services received, or other contractual documents. [AFIT]

OBLIGATION AUTHORITY Congressional or administrative authority to incur obligations; independent from the authority to make expenditures in payment thereof. [AFIT]

OBLIGATION OF FUNDS Legally binding commitments, such as contract awards, made by federal agencies during a given period that will require outlays during the same or some future period. [FAI]

OFFER (1) A legally binding promise, made by one party to another, to enter into a contractual agreement, if the offer is accepted. In sealed bidding, offers made in response to Invitations for Bids (IFBs) are called "bids." In negotiated acquisitions, offers made in response to Requests for Proposals (RFPs) are called "proposals." [FAI] (2) A proposal to make a contract. It is made orally, in writing, or by other conduct, and it must contain the terms legally necessary to create a contract. Acceptance of the proposal creates the contract. [FBL]

OFFICE OF FEDERAL PROCUREMENT POLICY (OFPP) An organization within the Office of Management and Budget (OMB) that provides leadership and direction to federal procurement programs. [FAI]

OFFICE OF MANAGEMENT AND BUDGET (OMB) A federal office that recommends and monitors federal programs and funding levels, develops and issues government-wide policy guidance on management concerns, and reviews proposed regulations. [FAI]

OFFSETS A cost balancing action whereby a claim may be canceled or lessened by a counterclaim. [L&P II]

OFF-THE-SHELF Procurement of existing systems or equipment without a research, development, test, and evaluation program or with minor development to make the system suitable for government needs. May be commercial system or equipment or a system or equipment already in the government's inventory. [DSMC] Also known as "Commercial-Off-The-Shelf." See also "Non-Developmental Item."

OLIGOPOLY A market dominated by a few sellers. [ECON]

OMB CIRCULAR A-76, PERFORMANCE OF COMMERCIAL ACTIVITIES A directive of the Office of Management and Budget that requires government-operated activities be contracted out whenever it is cost effective. [FAR]

OMB CIRCULAR A-109, MAJOR SYSTEMS ACQUISITION A directive of the Office of Management and Budget created as a result of the Commission on Government Procurement's recommendations that establishes policies to be followed by executive branch agencies in the acquisition of major systems. A "major system" is defined as a combination of elements that will function together to produce the capabilities required to fulfill a mission need. The circular states management objectives, management structure, and key decision points. [OMB]

OMB CIRCULAR A-120, GUIDELINES FOR THE USE OF ADVISORY AND ASSISTANCE SERVICES A directive of the Office of Management and Budget that specifically prohibits the government's use of advisory and assistance services obtained for professional or technical advice that is readily available within the government agency (except when the contract has been entered into and reviewed under the provisions of OMB Circular A-76, "Performance of Commercial Activities"). [TIPS(1-6)]

ON-LINE INSPECTION Any inspection or test that can be performed on an item without impeding the flow of the item through the receiving [or manufacturing] process. [AFIT]

OPEN END CONTRACT An agreement for the supply of goods or services that contains varying limits, or no limit, on time and quantity, and which usually involves recurring orders and changes of various types. [AFIT]

OPEN MARKET The collective name for private, commercial business sources of supplies and services. For example, in government small purchasing, open market sources can be used under two conditions: (1) no mandatory sources can meet the need; or (2) the open market can provide the same supplies or services at substantial savings. [FAI II]

OPPORTUNITY COST The maximum alternative earning that might have been obtained if the productive good, service, or capacity had been applied to some alternative use. [NCMA-CA]

OPTION A unilateral right in a contract by which, for a specified time, the government [buyer] may elect to purchase additional quantities of the supplies or services called for in the contract, or may elect to extend the period of performance of the contract. [AFIT]

ORDER OF PRECEDENCE A solicitation provision that establishes priorities so that contradictions within the solicitation can be resolved. [McVay]

ORGANIZATIONAL CONFLICT OF INTEREST (OCI) An organizational conflict of interest exists when the nature of the work to be performed under a proposed contract may, without some restriction on future activities, (a) result in an unfair competitive advantage to the contractor, or (b) impair the contractor's objectivity in performing the contract work. [FAR]

OUT YEARS The four fiscal years following the target years. [AFIT]

OUTLAYS Payments (e.g., checks issued, cash disbursed, and electronic fund transfers) by a federal department or agency. [FAI]

OVERHEAD An accounting cost pool that generally includes general indirect expenses that are necessary to operate a business but not directly accountable to a specific good or service produced. Some examples are building rent, utilities, salaries of corporate officers, janitorial services, office supplies and furniture, etc. [Navy]

OVERTIME Time worked by a contractor's employee in excess of the employee's normal workweek. [FAR]

OVERTIME PREMIUM The difference between the contractor's regular rate of pay to an employee for the shift involved and the higher rate paid for overtime. It does not include shift premium. [FAR]

— **P** —

PACKARD COMMISSION Established by the president in 1985 as the President's Blue Ribbon Commission on Defense Management, it is commonly called the "Packard Commission" in reference to its chairperson. The Commission was tasked to examine defense issues, cite problems, and recommend solutions. In June 1986, the Commission's final report, entitled *A Quest for Excellence*, was issued citing thirty-seven broadly worded recommendations. [TIPS(3-2)]

PARAMETRIC COST ESTIMATING Statistical and parametric estimating involves collecting and organizing historical information through mathematical techniques and relating this information to the work output being estimated. The format most commonly used for statistical and parametric estimating is the estimating relationship, which relates some physical characteristic of the work output (weight, power requirements, size, or volume) with the cost or labor-hours required to produce it. Estimating relationships have the advantage of providing a quick estimate even though very little is known about the work output except its physical characteristics. On the other hand, because of their dependence on past (historical) data, they may erroneously indicate cost trends. [CE]

PARTIAL PAYMENT A payment authorized under a contract, to be made upon completion of the delivery of one or more complete units called for, delivered, and accepted by the government [buyer] under the contract; also a payment made against a termination claim upon prior approval before final settlement of the total termination claim. [OPM]

PATENTS A government grant of exclusive rights to an inventor that prohibits others from making, using, or selling an invention. Usually valid for fifty years. [DOD]

PAYMENT See "Compensation Clause."

PAYMENT BOND A bond that assures payments as required by law to all persons supplying labor or material in the prosecution of the work provided for in the contract. A payment bond is required only when a performance bond is required, and if the use of a payment bond is in the government's [buyer's] interest. [FAR]

PECUNIARY LIABILITY The statutory obligation of an individual to reimburse the government for loss or improper application of funds or property. [AFIT]

PERFORMANCE "Performance" is the execution of the terms of a contract. If a buyer offers to purchase from a supplier, the supplier performs by furnishing the buyer's requirements. [FAI] Performance is an informal means of accepting an offer.

PERFORMANCE BOND A bond that secures the performance and fulfillment of all the undertakings, covenants, terms, conditions, and agreements contained in the contract. [AFIT]

PERFORMANCE MEASUREMENT BASELINE (PMB) The time-phased budget plan against which contract performance is measured. It is formed by the budgets assigned to scheduled cost accounts and the applicable indirect budgets. For future effort, not planned to the cost account level, the performance measurement baseline also includes budgets assigned to higher level Work Breakdown Structure (WBS) elements, and undistributed budgets. It equals the total allocated budget less management reserve. [JIG]

PERFORMANCE SPECIFICATION A purchase description that describes the deliverable in terms of desired operational characteristics. Performance specifications tend to be more restrictive than functional specifications, in terms of limiting alternatives that the government will consider and in terms of defining separate performance standards for each such alternative. [FAI]

PERIODIC INVENTORY METHOD An inventory accounting system that requires a physical count of inventory to determine the ending amounts of raw material, work in process, and finished goods, and, hence, also the costs of goods sold. [NCMA-CA]

PERPETUAL INVENTORY METHOD An inventory accounting system whereby a continuous record is kept that tracks raw materials, work in process, finished goods, and cost of goods sold on a day-to-day basis. [NCMA-CA]

PERSONAL SERVICES CONTRACT A contract that, by its express terms or as administered, makes the contractor personnel appear, in effect, as government employees. [FAI] In general, personal services contracts are illegal.

PHYSICAL CONFIGURATION AUDIT (PCA) A technical examination of a designated configuration item to verify that the item "as built" conforms to the technical documentation that defines the item. [DOD-MMH]

PILOT PRODUCTION A limited production run of a new system used to demonstrate the capability to mass produce an item. [AFIT] Also known as "Low Rate Initial Production."

PLANNING ESTIMATE The estimates of operational/technical characteristics, schedule, and program acquisition cost developed at the time of approval for program initiation. [AFIT]

PLANNING FACTOR An estimating relationship used to compute the amount and type of effort or resources that will be necessary to develop, produce, acquire, and/or operate a given system. [AFIT]

POINT OF FIRST RECEIPT Often referred to in discussions of "Fast Payment Procedure." The point of first receipt is designated by the government. It is the point where goods or services leave the supplier's hands, and from which they are forwarded to the eventual user. Post offices or common carriers are examples of such points. [FAI II]

POST-AWARD ORIENTATION A meeting of government [buyer] and contractor [supplier] personnel held soon after contract award to ensure that everyone understands the contract requirements. [McVay]

PRE-AWARD INQUIRY Questions and comments from prospective offerors about specifications, terms, and conditions in a solicitation received prior to the opening date of the IFB or closing date of the RFP. [FAI]

PRE-AWARD SURVEY An evaluation of a prospective contractor's ability to perform a specific contract, performed by the contract administration office or the purchasing office, with assistance from an audit organization at the request of either office. The evaluation addresses the physical, technical, managerial, and financial capability of the prospective contractor. Also addressed are the adequacy of the contractor's systems and procedures and past performance record. [L&P II]

PRE-BID CONFERENCE A conference held with prospective bidders in sealed-bid procurements prior to the submission of a bid to clarify any ambiguous situations, answer bidder questions, and ensure that all bidders have a common basis of understanding regarding the supplies or services required. Also known as a "Pre-proposal Conference" in a negotiated procurement. [OPM]

PREPRODUCTION INSPECTION Examination and testing performed, witnessed, or participated in by the government on one or more items submitted by a contractor to prove, prior to the initiation of production, that its production methods are capable of yielding items that comply with the technical requirements of the contract. [AFIT]

PREPROPOSAL CONFERENCE A meeting held with contractors after the Request for Proposals (RFPs) in negotiated procurements have been sent out. The goal is to promote uniform interpretation of work statements and specifications by all prospective contractors. [NCMA-SS]

See also "Pre-bid Conference."

PRESENT VALUE OF FUTURE CASH FLOWS A dollar today is worth more because of the interest cost. Thus, dollar benefits that accrue in the future cannot be compared directly with investments made in the present. Discounting is a technique for converting various cash flows occurring over time to equivalent amounts at a common point in time—considering the time value of money—to facilitate a valid comparison. [AFIT]

Also known as "Time Value of Future Cash Flows."

PRESIDENT'S BLUE RIBBON COMMISSION ON DEFENSE MANAGEMENT See "Packard Commission."

PRESOLICITATION CONFERENCE A meeting held with potential contractors or subcontractors prior to a formal solicitation, to discuss technical and other problems connected with a proposed procurement. The conference is also used to elicit the interest of prospective contractors in pursuing the task, such as an R&D effort. [DSMC]

PRICE (1) A monetary unit given, received, or asked for in exchange for supplies or services. [ASPM]
(2) The amount of money or equivalent paid or charged for supplies or services, including cost and profit or fee. [L&P]

PRICE ANALYSIS The process of examining and evaluating a prospective price without evaluation of the separate cost elements and proposed profit of the individual offeror. [OPM]

PRICE FIXING Any agreement, understanding, or arrangement among competitors to raise, lower, fix, or stabilize prices, as well as any agreement between a supplier and customer as to the price at which the customer may resell goods purchased. [BOE]

PRICE NEGOTIATION MEMORANDUM (PNM) The document that relates the story of the negotiation. A sales document establishing the reasonableness of the agreement reached with the successful offeror, as well as a permanent record of the decisions made by the negotiator in establishing that the price was fair and reasonable. [OPM]

PRICE VARIANCE The difference between the actual price and the standard price, multiplied by the total number of items acquired. The term "Price Variance" is usually linked with direct materials; the term "Rate Variance," which is conceptually similar to the price variance, is usually linked with direct labor. [NCMA-CA]

See also "Rate Variance."

PRICING ARRANGEMENT An agreed-to basis between contractual parties for the payment of amounts for specified performance; usually expressed in terms of a specific cost-reimbursement or fixed-price type arrangement. [OPM]

PRIME/PRIME CONTRACTOR The principal contractor performing under contract. Can include not only the principal, who acts as integrator or lead, but also major subcontractors teaming or performing in concert with the integrator. [DSMC]

PRIME COST The sum of direct material and direct labor. [NCMA-CA]

PRIOR COURSE OF DEALING An important type of extrinsic evidence used in the interpretive process to establish the meaning of ambiguous language. Also used to demonstrate that an explicit requirement of the contract is not binding because that requirement was not enforced in the past. [NC-A]

PRIORITY RATINGS "DO" and "DX" are the two types of priority ratings contained in the Defense Priorities and Allocations System (DPAS) Regulation that specify rules relating to the status, placement, acceptance, and treatment of priority-rated contracts and orders. "DO" ratings have equal preferential status and take priority over all unrated orders. "DX" ratings have equal preferential status and take priority over DO-rated and unrated orders. [Sherman]
See also "Defense Priorities and Allocations System."

PRIVITY OF CONTRACT (1) The direct legal (contractual) relationship that exists between parties that allows either party to (1) enforce contractual rights against the other party, and (2) seek remedy directly from the other party with whom this relationship exists. [L&P II]

(2) The legal relationship between two parties to the same contract. The government has "privity of contract" with the prime contractor. Therefore, the government's relationship with subcontractors is indirect in nature. Government involvement with subcontractors is channeled through prime contractor directed activities; only the prime contractor is authorized to direct the subcontractor. [DSMC]

PROBABILITY SAMPLING See "Sampling."

PROCEDURAL SUPPORT DATA Recorded procedures that are used by the contractor during the development program for assembly, operation, or maintenance tasks connected with production, testing, or inspection. [AFIT]

PROCESS A group of sequential, logically related tasks that use organizational resources to provide a product or a service to internal or external customers. [BOE II]

PROCESS CAPABILITY ANALYSIS A statistical technique used during development and production cycles to analyze the variability of a process relative to product specifications. [BOE II]

PROCESS COSTING A method of costing products with average costs computed on the basis of total costs divided by equivalent units of work performed. Usually used in high-volume, similar-product situations. [NCMA-CA]

PROCUREMENT The complete action or process of acquiring or obtaining goods or services using any of several authorized means. [AFIT]

PROCUREMENT AUTHORIZATION A document that establishes the approved material procurement program and authorizes and directs the action to be taken to place the approved material program under procurement. [AFIT]

PROCUREMENT AUTOMATED SOURCE SYSTEM (PASS) A centralized inventory and referral system containing the names and capabilities of small businesses interested in obtaining government contracts or subcontracts. [McVay]

PROCUREMENT, CATEGORIES OF The major categories of procurement are as follows: supplies; construction; services; and research and development. Within each of these major categories are numerous specialized types of procurement. The classification of the procurement is extremely important for purposes of funding, types of contracts to be used, applicability of contract clauses, and coverage of socioeconomic provisions. [NC-F]

PROCUREMENT LEAD TIME The time interval between the initiation of procurement and the receipt into the supply system of material purchased as a result of such action. [AFIT]
See also "Administrative Lead Time."

PROCUREMENT PACKAGE All information required to obtain bids or proposals; the technical information necessary to accurately describe the item to be procured. [AFIT]

PROCURING CONTRACTING OFFICER (PCO) The government agent designated by a warrant having the authority to obligate the government. The Procuring Contracting Officer (PCO) negotiates and signs the actual contractual document. Administration of the contract after award may be delegated to an Administrating Contracting Officer (ACO). [DSMC]

PRODUCT VERIFICATION INSPECTION Physical inspection or test of a product by the government after inspection and acceptance by the contractor's quality organization. [AFIT]

PRODUCTION READINESS REVIEW (PRR) A formal examination of a program to determine whether (1) the design is ready for production, (2) production engineering problems have been resolved, and (3) the producer has accomplished adequate planning for the production phase. [DOD-MMH]

PROFIT The net proceeds from selling a product or service when costs are subtracted from revenues. May be positive (profit) or negative (loss). [L&P] See also "Fee."

PROFIT CENTER The smallest organizationally independent segment of a company charged by the management with profit and loss responsibilities. [FAR]

PROFIT OBJECTIVE The part of the estimated contract price objective that the contracting officer concludes is appropriate for the procurement at hand. Developed after a thorough review of proposed contract work and all available knowledge regarding an offeror, as well as an analysis of the offeror's cost estimate and a comparison of it with the government's estimate or projection of cost. [OPM]

PROFITABILITY ACCOUNTING See "Responsibility Accounting."

PROGRAM EVALUATION AND REVIEW TECHNIQUE (PERT) One of the best known (along with the Critical Path Method, or CPM) techniques derived from the basic critical path scheduling concept. PERT emerged in 1958 through the joint efforts of the U.S. Navy; the Booz, Allen & Hamilton consulting firm; and the Lockheed Missile and Space Division in connection with the Polaris weapons program. With the passage of time, PERT and CPM have become very similar in concept. Currently, they differ only with respect to various details of application. In practice, the application of CPM/PERT generally is accomplished with a computer program. It uses network diagrams to show time and dependency relationships between the activities that make up the total project. The purpose of the technique is to keep all the "parts" arriving on schedule so that the total project can be completed as planned. [DBL]

PROGRAM MANAGER (PM) An individual charged with the responsibility for design, development, and acquisition of the system/equipment, and the design, development, and acquisition of the integrated logistic support. [AFIT]

PROGRESS PAYMENT A payment made as work progresses under a contract on the basis of percentage of completion accomplished, or for work performed at a particular stage of completion. [OPM]

PROMPT PAYMENT DISCOUNT A discount offered by a bidder for payment by the government [buyer] within a designated time period. [GUIDE]

PROPOSAL Normally, a written offer by a seller describing its offering terms. Proposals may be issued in response to a specific request or may be made unilaterally when a seller feels there may be an interest in its offer (which is also known as an "Unsolicited Proposal"). [Cohen]
See also "Offer" and "Unsolicited Proposal."

PROPOSAL EVALUATION An assessment of both the proposal and the offeror's ability (as conveyed by the proposal) to successfully accomplish the prospective contract. An agency shall evaluate competitive proposals solely on the factors specified in the solicitation. [FAR]
See also "Evaluation Factors."

PROPRIETARY INFORMATION Data owned by a contractor that is not publicly available, and which may be used only with the permission of the owner. [NCMA-SB]

PROSPECTIVE PRICING A pricing decision made in advance of performance, based on analysis of comparative prices, cost estimates, past costs, or combinations of such considerations. [OPM]

PROTEST A written objection by an interested party to a solicitation by an agency for offers for a proposed contract for the acquisition of supplies or services, or a written objection by an interested party to a proposed award or the award of such a contract. [FAR]

PROVISIONED ITEM A line item in the contract for which firm requirements (quantity or type) are not known at the time of contract preparation. A line item is therefore established for generic types of supplies or services, i.e., spare and repair parts, support equipment, engineering support, government property repair and data. Requirements for these line items are initiated by a requisition. [Navy]

PROVISIONING The process of determining or meeting the range and quantity of items required to support and maintain or function for a set period of time. [OPM]

PRUDENT BUSINESSPERSON CONCEPT Phrase used as a measure of reasonableness in assessing an offer or counteroffer or other action taken under a contract. Related to making a procurement decision based on sound fiduciary or business principles. [L&P II]

PURCHASE DESCRIPTION (1) A description of the essential physical characteristics and functions required to meet the government's [buyer's] minimum needs. [FAR]
(2) A simplified specification that is used when an item is purchased infrequently. [McVay]
See also "Purchase Order" and "Purchase Request."

PURCHASE ORDER (PO) A document, signed by a contracting officer and addressed to a contractor, requesting the future delivery of supplies, equipment, or material, or the future performance of nonpersonal services in accordance with certain terms in exchange for a promise by the government to pay the stated price. Considered an offer to contract rather than an acceptance of contract. [OPM]

PURCHASE REQUEST An exact description of a product or service, used in invitations for bids, requests for proposals, and contracts to tell prospective suppliers precisely what is required. [OPM]
Also known as a "Purchase Description."

PURCHASING (1) The process of buying supplies and services utilizing a variety of contractual arrangements. [L&P]
(2) In government, the process of buying readily available supplies and services utilizing procedures such as purchase orders, blanket purchase agreements, and prenegotiated schedules. [L&P]

QUALIFIED BIDDERS LIST (QBL) A list of bidders who have had their products examined and tested and who have satisfied all applicable qualification requirements for that product or have otherwise satisfied all applicable qualification requirements. [FAR]

QUALIFIED MANUFACTURERS LIST (QML) A list of manufacturers who have had their products examined and tested and who have satisfied all applicable qualification requirements for that product. [FAR]

QUALIFIED PRODUCT An item that has been examined and tested for compliance with specification requirements and qualified for inclusion in a qualified products list. [GUIDE]

QUALIFIED PRODUCTS LIST (QPL) A list of products that have been examined, tested, and have satisfied all applicable qualification requirements. [FAR]

QUALITY The composite of all attributes or characteristics, including performance, that satisfy a user's needs. [GAO]

QUALITY ASSURANCE A planned and systematic pattern of actions necessary to provide adequate confidence that material, data, supplies, and services conform to established technical requirements, and to achieve satisfactory performance. [AFIT]

QUALITY CONTROL The process of measuring quality performance, comparing it with the standard, and acting on the difference. [BOE II]

QUANTITY DISCOUNT A price reduction given to a buyer for purchasing increasingly larger quantities of materials. A quantity discount is normally offered (1) for purchasing a specific

quantity of items at one time; (2) for purchasing a specified dollar total at one time; or (3) for purchasing a specified dollar total over an agreed-upon time period (also known as a "Cumulative Discount"). [DBL]
See also "Trade Discount."

QUANTITY VARIANCE The standard price for a given resource, multiplied by the difference between the actual quantity used and the total standard quantity allowed for the number of good units produced. [NCMA-CA]

QUI TAM ACTION An action brought by an informer [sometimes known as a "Whistleblower"]. Part of the penalty goes to any person who brings such action and the remainder to the state or some other suit [e.g., the government]. Called a "Qui Tam Action" because the plaintiff states that he or she sues for the state as well as for him- or herself. [BLD]

QUOTATION A statement of price, either written or verbal, which may include among other things a description of the product or service; the terms of sale, delivery, or period of performance; and payment. Such statements are usually issued by sellers at the request of potential buyers. In federal government procurement, quotations do not constitute an offer that can be accepted to form the basis of a binding contract. Rather, quotations are solicited to obtain market information for planning purposes. [L&P II]

RATE VARIANCE The difference between actual wages paid and the standard wage rate, multiplied by the total actual hours of direct labor used. [NCMA-CA]
See also "Price Variance."

RATIFICATION In a broad sense, the confirmation of a previous act done either by the party itself or by another, as confirmation of a voidable act. The affirmance by a person of a prior act that did not bind him or her, but which was done or professedly done on his or her account, whereby the act, as to some or all persons, is given the effect as if originally authorized by him or her. [BLD]

REASONABLE COST A cost is reasonable if, in its nature and amount, it does not exceed that which would be incurred by a prudent person in the conduct of competitive business. [FAR]

RECIPROCITY An agreement or understanding that one company will buy goods or services from a supplier in exchange for the supplier's purchase of equipment, programs, or services from that company. [BOE]

RECURRING COSTS Costs that are required to operate and maintain an operation and that (1) vary or occur with the quantity being produced, and (2) occur repeatedly during the life cycle of a program, system, product, or service. [L&P II]

REGULAR DEALER A person that owns, operates, or maintains a store, warehouse, or other establishment in which the materials, supplies, articles, or equipment of the general character described by the specifications and required under the contract are bought, kept in stock, and sold to the public in the usual course of business. [FAR]
See also "Walsh-Healey Public Contracts Act."

RELIABILITY The duration or probability of failure-free performance under stated conditions. [DOD-MMH]

RENEGOTIATION BOARD Created as an independent establishment in the executive branch by the Renegotiation Act of 1951 (65 Stat. 7; 50 U.S.C.A. App 1211), and organized on October 8, 1951. The Board seeks the elimination of excessive profits on defense and space contracts and related subcontracts. This is accomplished through informal and nonadversary proceedings before the Board and its regional boards. Contractors not agreeing with Board determinations may petition the Court of Claims for redetermination. [BLD]

REPLEVIN A legal action whereby the owner of goods can legally recover them from someone who is holding them unlawfully. [FBL]

REQUEST FOR EQUITABLE ADJUSTMENT (REA) A letter or proposal from a contractor requesting a change to the contract price or schedule. [Navy]

REQUEST FOR PROPOSALS (RFP) Solicitation document used in negotiated procurement when the buyer reserves the right to award without further oral or written negotiation. Only the acceptance of the buyer is required to create a binding contract. Of course, the buyer can choose to negotiate further at its option. [DSMC]

REQUEST FOR QUOTATIONS (RFQ) The solicitation form used in negotiated procurement when award will be made after negotiation with the offeror. Since the prospective subcontractor's quotation is not a formal offer, the prime contractor and subcontractor must reach a bilateral negotiated agreement before a binding contract exists. [DSMC]

REQUEST FOR TECHNICAL PROPOSALS Solicitation document used in two-step sealed bidding. Normally in letter form, it asks only for technical information; price and cost breakdowns are forbidden. [DSMC]

REQUIREMENTS CONTRACT A type of contract that provides for the filling of all actual purchase requirements of specific supplies or services for a designated activity during a specified contract period. [OPM]

REQUISITION A request for supplies or services originating from the party actually requiring them. [FAI II]
See also "Purchase Request."

RESCISSION The unmaking of a contract, or an undoing of it from the beginning. Not merely a termination. It may be effected by mutual agreement of parties, or by one of the parties declaring rescission of contract without consent of other if a legally sufficient ground therefor exists. An action of equitable nature in which a party seeks to be relieved of its obligations under a contract on the grounds of mutual mistake, fraud, impossibility, etc. [BLD]

RESEARCH AND DEVELOPMENT (R&D) CONTRACT A contract for basic research (directed toward increasing knowledge), applied research (directed toward improving or expanding new scientific discoveries, technologies, materials, processes, or techniques), or development (directed production of, or improvements in, useful products to meet specific performance requirements through the systematic application of scientific knowledge). [OPM]

RESPONSIBILITY ACCOUNTING A system of accounting that recognizes various responsibilities throughout the organization and that reflects the plans and actions of each of these centers by allocating particular revenues and costs to the one having the pertinent responsibility. [NCMA-CA]
Also known as "Activity Accounting" and "Profitability Accounting."

RESPONSIBLE CONTRACTOR A capable party that has the financial resources, personnel, facilities, integrity, and overall capability to fulfill specific contractual requirements satisfactorily. [NCMA-SB]

RESPONSIVE (1) Describes a bid that meets, without any material deviation, the expressed requirements of a solicitation. [NCMA-SB]
(2) When a bidder fully complies with and does not materially deviate from the terms, conditions, and specifications set forth in an invitation for bids (sealed-bid method), it is deemed "responsive." [L&P]
(3) When an offeror materially complies with a solicitation and is capable of being made compliant through discussions, it is deemed "responsive." [L&P]

RESTRICTED COMPUTER SOFTWARE Computer software developed at private expense and that is a trade secret; is commercial or financial and confidential or privileged; or is published, copyrighted computer software, including minor modifications of such computer software. [FAR]

RESTRICTED RIGHTS A form of limited rights that applies only to computer software. Data protected under restricted rights is referred to as "restricted computer software." [TIPS(2-5)]
See "Rights in Technical Data."

RETURN ON INVESTMENT (ROI) A measure of income or profit divided by the investment required to help obtain the income or profit. That is, given the same risks, for any given amount of resources required, the investor wants the maximum income. [MGMT]

REVENUE RECOGNITION AND REALIZATION Generally accepted accounting principles state that revenue should be recognized (realized) when the earning process is virtually complete and an exchange has taken place. There are exceptions to this rule, particularly in the case of percentage-of-completion construction contracts where revenue is recognized over the life of the construction project. The purpose of the revenue realization principle is to provide an accurate representation of the economic substance of revenue-related transactions. [NCMA-CA]

REVERSE ENGINEERING Process whereby a product is analyzed to determine the composition of its various design elements for the purpose of producing a like product or performance capability. [L&P II]

RIGHTS IN TECHNICAL DATA The right for the government to acquire technical data. If the government has funded or will fund a part of or the entire development of the item, component, or process, then the government is entitled to unlimited rights in the technical data. However, if the above is developed by a contractor or subcontractor exclusively at private expense, the government is entitled to limited rights. Such data must be unpublished and identified as limited rights data. [DSMC]

See also "Government Purpose License Rights"; "Limited Rights"; "Restricted Rights"; and "Unlimited Rights."

RISK The probability of not attaining the goals for which the party entered into a contract. For the government, the principal risks are that
- the total cost of the acquisition will be higher than expected or unreasonable in relation to the actual costs of performance;
- the contractor will fail to deliver or will not deliver on time;
- the final deliverable will not satisfy the government's actual need, whether or not "acceptable" under the terms and conditions of the contract; and
- the government's need will change prior to receipt of the deliverable. [FAI]

RISK ASSESSMENT The process of subjectively determining the probability that a specific interplay of performance, schedule, and cost as an objective will or will not be attained along the planned course of action. [L&P II]

ROBINSON-PATMAN ACT Section 2(a) of the Clayton Act, as amended in 1936 by the Robinson-Patman Act (15 U.S.C.A. 13), makes it unlawful for any seller engaged in commerce to directly or indirectly discriminate in the price charged purchasers on the sale of commodities of like grade and quality where the effect may be to injure, destroy, or prevent competition with any person who grants or knowingly receives a discrimination, or the customer of either. [BLD]

RULE 4 FILE A file containing the contracting officer's final decision, the contract, pertinent correspondence, affidavits, and related information that is prepared pursuant to Rule 4 of the Rules of the Armed Services Board of Contract Appeals. [GUIDE]

— **S** —

SAFETY STOCK A minimum or buffer inventory as a cushion against reasonable expected maximum usage. The appropriate level of safety stock depends on the cost of running out of inventory versus the carrying cost of the safety stock. [MGMT]

SAMPLE SIZE Number of units to be selected for the random samples. [BOE II]

SAMPLING Method of obtaining statistics from a large body of data without resorting to a complete census of the data. Two broad methods of selecting samples are probability sampling (in which sample units are selected according to the law of chance) and nonprobability sampling (in which personal choice, expert judgment, or some other nonprobabilistic rationale is used to select sample units). [Cohen]

SCRAP (1) The loss of labor and material resulting from defects that cannot be economically repaired or used. [BOE II]

(2) Residual material resulting from machine or assembly processes, such as machine shavings, unusable lengths of wire, faulty parts. [DOD-MMH]
SEALED-BID PROCEDURE Formerly known as "Formal Advertising." A method of procurement involving the unrestricted solicitation of bids, a public opening, and award of a contract to the lowest responsible bidder. [NCMA-SB]
See also "Formal Advertising" and "Invitation for Bids."
SECOND SOURCE An acquisition strategy that establishes two or more producers for the same part, system, or service for the purpose of increasing competition or broadening the industrial base. [L&P II]
SECTION 8(a) SUBCONTRACT A subcontract between the Small Business Administration and a socially and economically disadvantaged business concern. [NCMA-SC]
Named after the section of the Small Business Act that authorized it. [TIPS(2-9)]
SEPARABLE COST A cost directly identifiable with a particular segment. [NCMA-CA]
SERVICE CONTRACT A contract for the time and services of individuals or organizations in support of a government objective. [OPM]
See also "Contracting Out."
SERVICE CONTRACT ACT Federal law establishing labor standards for such matters as wages and working conditions, which applies to every government contract over $2,500 when its principal purpose is to furnish services to the government. [GUIDE]
SET ASIDE A kind or class of procurement reserved for contenders that fit a certain category (e.g., business size, region, minority status). [OPM]
SETTLEMENT PROPOSAL A proposal for effecting settlement of a contract terminated in whole or in part. [FAR]
SEVERABLE CONTRACT A contract divisible into separate parts; a default of one section does not invalidate the whole contract. [FBL]
SHERMAN ANTITRUST ACT The Sherman Antitrust Act (15 U.S.C.A. 1-7) prohibits any unreasonable interference, by contract, or combination, or conspiracy, with the ordinary, usual,
and freely competitive pricing or distribution system of the open market in interstate trade. [BLD]
See also "Clayton Act" and "Robinson-Patman Act."
SHIFT PREMIUM The difference between the contractor's regular rate of pay to an employee and the higher rate paid for extra-pay-shift work. [FAR]
SHOULD COST An estimate of what an item or system should cost based upon an evaluation by independent reviewers of all applicable contractor business methods (contrasting more efficient methods with present contractor methods). This evaluation should include subcontractor procedures when subcontracting is part of the proposal. The result is utilized to develop realistic price objectives for contract negotiation purposes. [L&P]
SHOW CAUSE LETTER A written delinquency notice informing a contractor of failure to perform within the specified terms of the contract, and advising that the government is considering termination for default. Affords the contractor the opportunity to show cause why it should not be terminated. [OPM]
See also "Default Termination."
SHRINKAGE An additional quantity of material added to the quantity listed on the Bill of Materials (BOM) to provide for spoilage, scrap, waste, and natural attrition. [DOD-MMH]
See also "Attrition."
SIMPLIFIED PROCEDURES Methods for entering into contracts without using elaborate and formal solicitation techniques (i.e., IFBs and RFPs). Restricted to purchases under the small purchase threshold (currently set at $25,000). [McVay]
SINGLE SOURCE One source among others in a competitive marketplace which, for justifiable reason, is found to be most advantageous for the purpose of contract award. [OPM]
SMALL AND DISADVANTAGED BUSINESS (SDB) CONCERNS A business whose size meets government size requirements for its particular industry type, or a business owned (at least 51 percent) by members of socially and economically disadvantaged groups (i.e., groups that have been subjected

to racial or ethnic prejudice or cultural bias). [OPM]

SMALL AND DISADVANTAGED BUSINESS UTILIZATION SPECIALIST (SADBUS) An advocate for small, minority, and women-owned businesses who is located at each military and civilian activity that has a procurement office. [McVay]

SMALL BUSINESS ACT (SBA) The Small Business Act (15 U.S.C. 631 et seq.) is a federal law providing preferences for small and small disadvantaged businesses in government contracting. [GUIDE]

SMALL BUSINESS ADMINISTRATION (SBA) The government agency whose function is to aid, counsel, provide financial assistance to, and protect the interests of the small business community. [McVay]

SMALL BUSINESS CONCERN A business that is independently owned and operated, and is not dominant in its field; a business concern meeting government size standards for its particular industry type. [OPM]

SMALL BUSINESS INNOVATION RESEARCH (SBIR) PROGRAM A program that requires federal agencies with research and development budgets in excess of $100 million to set aside a fixed percentage of their budgets exclusively for small business participation. [McVay]

SMALL PURCHASE PROCEDURES Actions involved in the purchasing, rental, or lease of supplies or services as an exception to the statutory requirement to procure by means of formal advertising in order to assure rapid delivery of a large volume of purchases, reduce administrative costs and paperwork, and improve opportunities for small and disadvantaged business concerns. Includes imprest fund (cash) actions, purchase orders, orders under blanket purchase agreements, or orders issued under federal supply schedules. [OPM]

SOCIOECONOMIC PROGRAMS Programs designed to benefit particular groups. They represent a multitude of program interests and objectives unrelated to procurement objectives. Some examples of these are preferences for small businesses and for American products, required sources for specified items, and minimum labor pay levels mandated for contractors. [Sherman2]

SOLE SOURCE ACQUISITION A contract for the purchase of supplies or services that is entered into or proposed to be entered into after soliciting and negotiating with only one source. [FAR]

SOLICITATION A document requesting or inviting offerors to submit offers. Solicitations basically consist of (1) a draft contract, and (2) provisions on preparing and submitting offers. [FAI]

SOURCE DATA Data generated in the course of research, development, design engineering, and production of systems, material, and services. [AFIT]

SOURCE SELECTION The process wherein the requirements, facts, recommendations, and policies relevant to an award decision in a competitive procurement of a system/project are examined and the decision made. [DSMC]

SOURCE SELECTION ADVISORY COUNCIL A group of people who are appointed by the Source Selection Authority (SSA). The Council is responsible for reviewing and approving the source selection plan (SSP) and the solicitation of competitive awards for major and certain less-than-major procurements. The Council also determines what proposals are in the competitive range and provides recommendations to the SSA for final selection. [Navy]

SOURCE SELECTION AUTHORITY (SSA) The person that makes the final source selection in a competition. The SSA is responsible for ensuring that the entire source selection process is properly and efficiently conducted. [Navy]

SOURCE SELECTION EVALUATION BOARD (SSEB) A group of personnel representing the various functional and technical disciplines relevant to the acquisition whose function is to evaluate proposals and report its findings. [NCMA-SS]

SOURCE SELECTION PLAN The document that describes the selection criteria, the process, and the organization to be used in evaluating proposals for competitively awarded contracts. [Navy]

SPEARIN DOCTRINE A rule that takes its name from a 1918 Supreme Court case. The case stated that by providing the contractor with specifications to be

followed in carrying out the contract work, the government impliedly warrants that, if the contractor complies with those specifications, an adequate result will follow. [BP(91-8)]
Also known as "Implied Warranty of Specifications."

SPECIAL TEST EQUIPMENT Either single or multipurpose integrated test units engineered, designed, fabricated, or modified to accomplish special purpose testing in performing a contract. It consists of items or assemblies of equipment that are interconnected and interdependent so as to become a new functional entity for special testing purposes. [FAR]

SPECIAL TOOLING Jigs, dies, fixtures, molds, patterns, taps, gauges, other equipment and manufacturing aids, all components of these items, and replacement of these items, which are of such a specialized nature that without substantial modification or alteration their use is limited to the development or production of particular supplies or parts thereof to the performance of particular services. [FAR]

SPECIFICATION A description of the technical requirements for a material, product, or service that includes the criteria for determining that the requirements have been met. [NCMA-SP]
There are generally three types of specifications used in government contracting: performance, functional, and design. [FAR]
See also "Spearin Doctrine."

SPLIT-OFF POINT See "Joint Products Costs."

SPOILAGE A form of waste material resulting from misuse of material or errors in workmanship. [DOD-MMH]

STANDARD A document that establishes engineering and technical limitations and applications of items, materials, processes, methods, designs, and engineering practices. It includes any related criteria deemed essential to achieve the highest practical degree of uniformity in materials or products, or interchangeability of parts used in those products. [FAR]
See also "Voluntary Standard."

STANDARD ABSORPTION COSTING That type of product costing in which the cost of the finished unit is calculated as the sum of the standard allowances for the factors of production, without reference to the costs actually incurred. [NCMA-CA]

STANDARD COST A cost determined to represent an expected value; a goal or baseline that is used to expedite the costing of transactions, determined from historical experience or contrived from the best information available. Excepting costs attributable to precise and highly predictable operations, actual costs will almost always vary from standard costs due to factors (usually called variances) that affect performance, such as employee fatigue, unforeseen interruptions, and other delays. [Cohen]

STANDARD DIRECT COSTING That type of product costing in which the cost of the finished unit is calculated as the sum of the costs of the standard allowance for the factors of production, excluding fixed factory overhead, which is treated as a period cost, and without reference to the costs actually incurred. [NCMA-CA]

STANDARD FORM (SF) A set of standard provisions or terms issued for use by all government agencies in regard to procurement matters. [GUIDE]

STANDARD HOURS ALLOWED (EARNED OR WORKED) The number of standard hours that are chargeable to production for the actual goods produced. [NCMA-CA]

STANDARDIZATION, INDUSTRIAL The process of establishing agreement on uniform identifications for definite characteristics of quality, design, performance, quantity, service, etc. A uniform identification is called a "Standard." [DBL]

STATEMENT OF WORK (SOW) That portion of a contract describing the actual work to be done by means of specifications or other minimum requirements, quantities, performance date, and a statement of the requisite quality. [DSMC]

STATIC BUDGET A budget prepared for only one level of activity and, consequently, one that does not adjust automatically to changes in the level of volume. [NCMA-CA]

STATISTICAL PROCESS CONTROL (SPC) The application of statistical methods to monitor variation in a pro-

cess over time. SPC displays variation in a process to identify special/assignable causes of variation versus common/chance causes of variation. [BOE II]
STATUTE A law enacted by the legislative branch of government and signed by the president. Identifiable by a Public Law (P.L.) number. [FAI]
STATUTE OF LIMITATIONS A statute that sets limits to the time in which a lawsuit may be filed in certain causes of action. [FBL]
STEVENSON-WYDLER TECHNOLOGY INNOVATION ACT This Act (P.L. 96-480) emphasized a national policy of transferring technology from federal laboratories to industry by setting aside 0.5 percent of each agency's research budget to fund technology transfer. [TIPS(1-14)]
STOCKLESS PURCHASING See "Systems Contract."
SUBCONTRACT A contract between a buyer and a seller in which a significant part of the supplies or services being obtained is for eventual use in a government [prime] contract. [DSMC]
SUBCONTRACT DATA REQUIREMENTS LIST (SCDRL) See "Contract Data Requirements List."
SUBCONTRACTING MANAGEMENT A concept that addresses subcontracting issues and the government's [buyer's] role in ensuring successful prime contractor interaction with subcontractors in order to satisfy prime contract requirements. [DSMC]
SUBCONTRACTOR A contractor that enters into a contract with a prime contractor or a subcontractor of the prime contractor. [DSMC]
SUBSTANTIAL PERFORMANCE Doctrine that prohibits termination of a contract for default if a contractor's performance deviates only in minor respects from the contract's requirements. [GUIDE]
SUNK COST A cost that has already been incurred and which, therefore, is irrelevant to the decision-making process. [NCMA-CA]
See also "Historical Cost."
SUPERIOR KNOWLEDGE Government liability for nondisclosure of information is based on an implied duty to disclose information that is vital for the preparation of estimates or for contract performance. This implied duty is consistent with the general contract law concepts of good faith and fair dealing. The contractor must show that the government possessed the undisclosed information. Knowledge of one government agency will not be attributed to another government agency absent some meaningful connection between the agencies. [NC-A]
SUPPLEMENTAL AGREEMENT Any contract modification that is accomplished by the mutual action of the parties. [OPM]
SUPPLIER The individual or concern actually performing services, or manufacturing, producing, and shipping any supplies required by the contract or subcontract. [AFIT]
SURETY An individual or corporation legally liable to the debt, default, or failure of a principal to satisfy a contractual obligation. [FAR]
SURPLUS Those materials that are in excess of a firm's operational requirements. Surpluses typically originate from three primary sources: (1) scrap and waste; (2) surplus, obsolete, or damaged stocks; and (3) surplus, obsolete, or damaged equipment. [DBL]
SURPLUS, DISPOSAL OF When material is declared surplus, the materials management, purchasing, or other such department, as appropriate, is informed. Following this action, disposal is made by one of seven methods: (1) use within the firm; (2) return to the supplier; (3) direct sale to another firm; (4) sale to a dealer or broker; (5) sale to employees; (6) donations to educational institutions; or (7) some combination of the preceding. [DBL]
SUSPENSION Action taken by a suspending official to disqualify a contractor temporarily from government contracting and subcontracting. [FAR]
SUSPENSION OF WORK CLAUSE Allows the buyer the right to temporarily halt the work. May provide a maximum time period for such suspension. [Cohen]
SYNOPSIS An abbreviated description of a procurement that is published in the Commerce Business Daily in advance of the procurement, along with the contracting officer's name, for the purpose of informing the commercial world of

the opportunity to bid or submit an offer. [OPM]

SYSTEM The organization of hardware, software, material, facilities, personnel, data, and services needed to perform a designated function with specified results, such as the gathering of specified data, its processing, and delivery to users. Or a combination of two or more interrelated equipments (sets) arranged in a functional package to perform an operational function or to satisfy a requirement. [DSMC]

SYSTEM ACQUISITION PROCESS The sequence of acquisition activities starting from an organization's delineation of its requirement needs, with its capabilities, priorities and resources, and extending through the introduction of a system into operational use. [DSMC]

SYSTEM ENGINEERING The application of scientific and engineering efforts to transform an operational need into a description of a system configuration that best satisfies the operational need according to the measures of effectiveness; integrates related technical parameters; assures compatibility of all physical, functional, and technical program interfaces in a manner optimizing the total system definition and design; and integrates the efforts of all engineering disciplines and specialties into the total engineering effort. [DSMC]

SYSTEMS CONTRACT A contract that authorizes designated employees of the buying firm, using a predetermined release system, to place orders directly with the supplier for specified materials during a given contract period. One principal objective of systems contracting is to reduce the buyer's inventories to a level as low as is consistent with assured continuity of supply; thus, systems contracting is sometimes referred to as "Stockless Purchasing." Order releases under systems contracts should usually be made by personnel from the using department. [DBL]

TAILORING The process by which individual sections, paragraphs, or sentences of a specification or solicitation are modified to meet the minimum requirements and specific needs of the requestor. [NCMA-SP]

TARGET FISCAL YEAR The fiscal year two fiscal years into the future from the current fiscal year; the year for detailed consideration in programming. [AFIT]

TAX ACCOUNTING Involves the measuring, recording, and reporting of relevant financial information in accordance with tax rules and regulations to interested users (primarily government authorities). [NCMA-CA]

TEAM ARRANGEMENT An arrangement in which either (a) two or more companies form a partnership or joint venture to act as a potential prime contractor; or (b) a potential prime contractor agrees with one or more other companies to have them act as its subcontractors under a specified government contract or acquisition program. [FAR]

TECHNICAL ANALYSIS Evaluation, ordinarily conducted by engineering, technical, or specialized personnel, of the (1) technical and managerial qualifications of a contractor to perform a particular contract requirement, and (2) applicability/sufficiency of the technical solution proposed to fulfill contemplated contract requirements. [L&P II]

TECHNICAL DATA Recorded information, regardless of the form or method of the recording, of a scientific or technical nature (including computer software documentation). [DSMC]

TECHNICAL DATA PACKAGE Those documents, drawings, reports, manuals, revisions, technical orders, or other submissions as set forth as a Contract Data Requirements List (CDRL) line item to be delivered as required by contract. [DOD-MMH]

TECHNICAL FACTORS Factors other than price-related used in evaluating offers for award. Examples include technical excellence, management capability, personnel qualifications, prior experience, past performance, and schedule compliance. [FAI]

TECHNICAL LEVELING Helping an offeror to bring its proposal up to the level of other proposals through successive rounds of discussion, such as by pointing out weaknesses resulting from the offeror's lack of diligence, competence, or inventiveness in preparing the proposal. This practice is not allowed in federal government contracting. [FAR]

TECHNICAL TRANSFUSION Disclosure of technical information pertaining to a proposal that results in improvement of a competing proposal. This practice is not allowed in federal government contracting. [FAR]

TECHNOLOGY TRANSFER The process by which federal scientific research and development is transformed into commercially viable products and services. [TIPS(1-14)]

TERMINATION An action taken pursuant to a contract clause in which the contracting officer unilaterally ends all or part of the work; can be "Termination for Convenience," in which the ending of work is in the best interest of the government, or "Termination for Default," in which the contractor has not performed according to the terms of the contract. [OPM] See also "Convenience Termination" and "Default Termination."

TERMINATION CLAIM Any claim or demand by a prime contractor for compensation because of the termination before completion of any contract or subcontract for the convenience of the government. [AFIT]

TERMINATION CONTRACTING OFFICER (TCO) The contracting officer assigned responsibility for settling terminations for default or convenience, and in some cases settling claims and actions involving extraordinary relief. [OPM]

TERMINATION INVENTORY Any property purchased, supplied, manufactured, furnished, or otherwise acquired for the performance of a contract subsequently terminated and properly allocable to the terminated portion of the contract. It includes government-furnished property. It does not include facilities, material, special test equipment, or special tooling that are subject to a separate contract or to a special contract requirement governing their use or disposition. [FAR]

TERMS AND CONDITIONS All language in a contract, including time of delivery, packing and shipping, applicable standard clauses, and special provisions. [OPM]

TESTING (1) The determination by technical means of the physical and chemical properties or elements of materials, supplies, or components, involving not so much the element of personal judgment as the application of established scientific principles and procedures. [AFIT]
(2) An element of inspection. [DOD-MMH]

THEN-YEAR DOLLARS See "Current Year Dollars."

TIME AND MATERIALS CONTRACTS A type of contract providing for a fixed hourly rate, including overhead and profit and material at cost plus handling charges. Used when it is impossible to estimate schedule and costs at the time of contract award. [OPM]

TIME VALUE OF FUTURE CASH FLOWS See "Present Value of Future Cash Flows."

TORNCELLO RULE In *Torncello v. United States* (1982), the Court ruled that the Termination for Convenience clause could not be used to avoid anticipated profits, unless there had been some change in circumstances between the time of award of the contract and the time of termination. [NC-A]

TOTAL COST BASIS A means of pricing equitable adjustments when the costs associated with a claim are not clearly identifiable. Using the total cost approach, an equitable adjustment is calculated as the difference between the contractor's proposed price on the original contract and the actual total cost of performing the contract as changed. [TIPS(2-12)]

TOTAL QUALITY MANAGEMENT (TQM) The government term for the philosophy and principles that guide a continuously improving organization. It is the application of quantitative methods and human resources to improve the material and services supplied to an organization, the processes within an organization, and the degree to which the needs of the customer are met. [BOE II]

TRADE AGREEMENTS ACT The Trade Agreements Act of 1979 (19 U.S.C. 2501-2582) specifically prohibits the purchase of end product items from nondesignated countries, as determined by the U.S. Trade Representative. In particular, federal agencies are currently prohibited from procurements with certain Communist Areas and with certain Sanctioned Persons. [TIPS(1-15)]

TRADE DISCOUNT A discount from list price offered to all customers of a given type; e.g., discount offered by lumber dealer to building contractor. Contrast with a discount offered for prompt payment or a quantity discount. [BLD]

TRADE SECRET A form of legal protection for any information used in a commercial trade or business that (1) is not generally known in the trade; (2) is used in secrecy; and (3) affords a competitive advantage. The Trade Secrets Act (18 U.S.C.S. 1905) restricts disclosure of trade secrets, and provides for civil and criminal penalties for violations. A company does not need to request "trade secret" status from anyone. Rather, it can declare such a status by adhering to certain practices. [TIPS(2-5)]

TRANSPORTATION, MODES OF Transportation is a means of moving freight traffic. A surprisingly large number of transportation methods are available: parcel post; private parcel delivery service; bus service; air cargo; rail freight, CarLoad (CL), and Less-than-CarLoad (LCL); motor freight, TruckLoad (TL), and Less-than-Truck-Load (LTL); freight forwarder; coastal, intercoastal, and inland water freight; piggyback and fishyback; and pipeline. [DBL]

TREASURY MEMORANDUM ACCOUNT See "'M' Account."

TRUTH IN NEGOTIATIONS ACT (TINA) Federal law enacted as P.L. 87-653 to provide the government with sufficient information prior to contract award to ensure that it does not pay excessive prices for its procurements, which requires contractors to submit cost or pricing data and to certify that, to the contractor's best knowledge and belief, the data submitted is accurate, complete, and current. [GUIDE]

THE 1207 PROGRAM Named after the section of the DOD Appropriations Act of 1987 that authorized it, this program allows DOD to "set aside" contracts for socially and economically disadvantaged firms. The program also allows DOD to apply a 10 percent evaluation preference when awarding a contract to a socially and economically disadvantaged business that competes in unrestricted procurements. [TIPS(2-9)]

TWO-STEP SEALED BIDDING A combination of competitive procedures designed to obtain the benefits of sealed bidding when adequate specifications are not available. An objective is to permit the development of a sufficiently descriptive and not unduly restrictive statement of the government's requirements, including an adequate technical data package, so that subsequent acquisitions may be made by conventional sealed bidding. This method is especially useful in acquisitions requiring technical proposals, particularly those for complex items. Step one consists of the request for submission of technical proposals, evaluation, and discussions without pricing. Step two involves the submission of sealed-priced bids by those who submitted acceptable technical proposals in step one. [FAR]

TYING AGREEMENTS An agreement or understanding to sell a desired product upon the condition that the customer must buy another of the supplier's products. [BOE]

UNALLOWABLE COST Any cost that, under the provisions of any pertinent law, regulation, or contract, cannot be included in prices, cost-reimbursements, or settlements under a government contract to which it is allocable. [FAR]

UNCOMPENSATED OVERTIME Work that exempt employees perform above and beyond forty hours per week. [OPM] Also known as "Competitive Time"; "Deflated Hourly Rates"; "Direct Allocation of Salary Costs"; "Discounted Hourly Rates"; "Extended Work Week"; "Full-time Accounting"; and "Green Time." [TIPS(2-11)]

UNCONSCIONABILITY Basic test of "unconscionability" of contract is whether, under circumstances existing at the time of making of contract and in light of general commercial background and the commercial needs of a particular trade or case, clauses involved are so one-sided as to oppress or unfairly surprise party. Unconscionability is generally recognized to include an absence of meaningful choice on the part of one of the parties to a contract, together with contract terms that are unreasonably favorable to the other party. Typically, the cases in which unconscionability is found involve gross overall one-sidedness or gross one-sidedness of a term disclaiming a warranty, limiting damages, or granting procedural advantages. [BLD]

UNDEFINITIZED CONTRACT ACTION Any contract action for which the contract terms, specifications, or price are not agreed upon before performance is begun under the action. [Navy]

UNEXPIRED COST A cost that may be properly carried forward to future periods as an asset to measure. [NCMA-CA]

UNIFORM COMMERCIAL CODE (UCC) Uniform law governing commercial transactions, developed by the National Conference of Commissioners on Uniform State Laws and the American Law Institute, which has been adopted by all states in the U.S. except Louisiana, and which is sometimes used to aid in the interpretation and enforcement of government subcontracts. [GUIDE]

UNIFORM CONTRACT FORMAT The format (Section A through Section M) that must be used in most Invitations for Bids and Requests for Proposals. [McVay]
   The uniform contract format is as follows:
Part I—The Schedule:
- Section A—Solicitation/contract form
- Section B—Supplies or services and prices
- Section C—Description/specifications
- Section D—Packaging and marking
- Section E—Inspection and acceptance
- Section F—Deliveries or performance
- Section G—Contract administration data
- Section H—Special contract requirements

Part II—Contract Clauses:
- Section I—Contract clauses

Part III—List of documents, exhibits, and other attachments:
- Section J—List of documents, exhibits, and other attachments

Part IV—Representations, certifications, and other statements of bidders:
- Section K—Representations, certifications, and other statements of bidders
- Section L—Instructions, conditions, and notices to bidders
- Section M—Evaluation factors for award [FAR]

UNILATERAL Means that the contracting officer [buyer] does something without the concurrence of the contractor. For example, a unilateral modification would be a change to a contract where the PCO signs but the contractor does not. Unilateral modifications are used for the following:
- making administrative changes;
- issuing change orders;
- making changes authorized by clauses other than the Changes clause (e.g., Options clause, Property clause, etc.); and
- issuing termination notices. [Navy]

UNILATERAL CONTRACT See "Bilateral Contract."

UNIT COST A total cost divided by some related base, such as labor hours, machine-hours, or units of product. [NCMA-CA]

UNITED STATES COURT OF APPEALS FOR THE FEDERAL CIRCUIT Federal court that, upon dissolution of the U.S. Court of Claims in 1982, assumed the role of the Court of Claims' appellate division. [GUIDE]

UNITED STATES COURT OF CLAIMS Until its dissolution in 1982, the federal court that resolved most government contract disputes brought in federal court. [GUIDE]

UNITED STATES SUPREME COURT Highest of all federal courts that can review a government contracts case, but which does so very infrequently, reserving review primarily for cases involving important questions with far-ranging implications. [GUIDE]

UNJUST ENRICHMENT Where one of the parties to the contract receives benefits far in excess of the amount of money involved. [Cohen]

UNLIMITED RIGHTS Rights to use, duplicate, release, or disclose technical data or computer software in whole or in part in any manner and for any purpose and to have or permit others to do so. [DSMC]
See "Rights in Technical Data."

UNRESTRICTED PROCUREMENT Those acquisitions available to all contractors, and not reserved to satisfy social or economic programs of the federal government. [TIPS(2-9)]

UNSOLICITED PROPOSAL A research or developmental proposal that is made by a prospective contractor without prior formal or informal solicitation from a purchasing activity. [AFIT]

VALIDATION Acceptance by auditors of reported cost reduction savings and cost reduction reports, based on a selective review of cost reduction reports and supporting documentation. [AFIT]

VALUE ANALYSIS A systematic and objective evaluation of the function of a product and its related cost; a pricing tool that provides insight into the inherent worth of a product. [OPM]

VALUE ENGINEERING (VE) An organized effort directed at analyzing the function of systems, subsystems, equipment, facilities, procedures, and supplies for the purpose of achieving the required function at the lowest total cost consistent with performance, reliability, quality, maintainability, and producibility. [AFIT]

VALUE ENGINEERING CHANGE PROPOSAL (VECP) A proposal that requires a change to the contract to implement and results in reducing the overall projected cost to the agency without impairing essential functions or characteristics, provided that it does not involve a change in deliverable end item quantities, R&D quantities, or the contract type. [FAR]

VARIABLE BUDGET See "Flexible Budget."

VARIABLE COST A cost that changes with the rate of production of goods or performance of services. [OPM]

VARIABLE COSTING See "Direct Costing."

VARIANCE The difference between projected and actual performance, especially relating to costs. [AFIT]
See also "Standard Cost."

VENDOR An individual, partnership, corporation, or other entity from whom items are acquired in the performance of a contract. [AFIT]

VISUAL ANALYSIS The visual inspection of an item or its drawings, from which a general estimate of probable value may be made. [AFIT]

VOLUNTARY DISCLOSURE PROGRAM Created in April 1990 for the DOD, this program offers a means by which defense contractors can identify their own potential civil or criminal fraud violations. In return for this disclosure, the DOD generally grants the contractor the opportunity to conduct an internal investigation, which the government later verifies. The DOD agrees not to pursue administrative actions until its verification process is completed. [TIPS(3-2)]

VOLUNTARY STANDARD A standard established by a private sector body and available for public use. The term does not include private standards of individual firms. [FAR]

WAGE AND CLASSIFICATION Guidelines to be used by the contracting office in determining applicable wages for specific classes of employees expected to be employed by the contractor to perform the required services under a proposed service contract. Determinations are made by the Department of Labor in accordance with the Service Contract Act. [OPM]

WAIVER (1) The voluntary relinquishment by a person of a right that he or she has. [FBL]
(2) Acceptance by the government [buyer] of a minor nonconformity that does not degrade the function of the item. [McVay]

WALSH-HEALEY PUBLIC CONTRACTS ACT A law (41 U.S.C. 35-45) that requires a contractor that furnishes supplies to the government to be either a manufacturer or regular dealer of the supplies. Includes stipulations on minimum wages, maximum hours, labor practices, and working conditions. [FAR]

WARNER AMENDMENT Another name for 10 U.S.C. 2315, which exempts the Department of Defense from the Brooks Act for certain applications. Under the Warner Amendment, the Brooks Act does not apply when DOD acquires ADPE for the following: intelligence activities; cryptologic activities related to national security; command and control of military forces; an integral part of a weapon or weapon system; or a critical component for the direct fulfillment of a military or intelligence mission. [TIPS(3-3)]

WARRANT A contracting officer's certificate of appointment. [McVay]

WARRANTY A promise or affirmation given by a seller to a buyer regarding the nature, usefulness, or condition of the supplies or performance of services furnished under the contract. Generally, a warranty's purpose is to delineate the rights and obligations for defective items and services, and to foster quality performance. [NES92]

WARRANTY, EXPRESS A written statement arising out of a sale to the consumer of a consumer good, pursuant to which the manufacturer, distributor, or retailer undertakes to preserve or maintain the utility or performance of the consumer good or provide compensation if there is a failure in utility or performance. It is not necessary to the creation of an express warranty that formal words such as "warrant" or "guarantee" be used, or that a specific intention to make a warranty be present. [BLD]

WARRANTY, IMPLIED A promise arising by operation of law, that something that is sold shall be merchantable and fit for the purpose for which the seller has reason to know that it is required. Some types of implied warranties are as follows: implied warranty of fitness for a particular purpose, implied warranty of merchantability, implied warranty of title, and implied warranty of wholesomeness. [BLD]
See also "Spearin Doctrine."

WEIGHTED AVERAGE COST METHOD A method of determining the average unit cost of inventory, and by implication an aid in determining the cost of goods made, sold, or held for future sale or incorporation into higher level end items. Under this technique, costs are periodically computed by adding the sum of the costs of beginning inventory with the sum of the costs of subsequent purchases, and dividing by the total number of units. [L&P II]

WEIGHTED GUIDELINES METHOD (WGM) A cost analysis technique used to ensure consideration of the relative value of appropriate profit factors in establishing profit objectives and conducting negotiations. Used as a basis for documentation and explaining final pricing factors, including contractor's input to total contract performance, contractor's assumption of contract risk, record of contractor's performance, and other selected factors. [OPM]

WHISTLEBLOWER See "Qui Tam Action."

WILL COST (1) A concept of contract pricing that requires an evaluation of what an offeror estimates it will cost to do the job in a specified future period. [OPM]
(2) A projection by an offeror as to what a contract will cost, based upon the offeror's best estimate utilizing current methods, historical costs, and forecasts. [L&P]

WORK BREAKDOWN STRUCTURE (WBS) A product-oriented family tree division of hardware, software, services, and other work tasks. It organizes, defines, and graphically displays the product to be produced, as well as the work to be accomplished to achieve the specified product. [DSMC]

WORK-IN-PROCESS INVENTORY The cost of uncompleted goods still on the production line. [NCMA-CA]

WORK PACKAGES Detailed short-span jobs, or material items, identified by the contractor for accomplishing work required to complete the contract. A work package has the following characteristics:
- it represents units of work at levels where work is performed;
- it is clearly distinguished from all other work packages;
- it is assignable to a single organizational element;
- it has scheduled start and completion dates and, as applicable, interim milestones, all of which are representative of physical accomplishment;
- it has a budget or assigned value expressed in terms of dollars, man-hours, or other measurable units;
- its duration is limited to a relatively short span of time, or it is subdivided by discrete value milestones to facilitate the objective measurement of work performed; and
- it is integrated with detailed engineering, manufacturing, or other schedules. [JIG]

ZERO-BASE BUDGETING (ZBB) An elaborate, time-consuming practice of having managers justify all their activities and costs as if they were being undertaken for the first time. ZBB is successfully used in many nonprofit organizations because most costs in many nonprofit organizations are discretionary. ZBB forces managers to define the output of various programs of expenditures and relate inputs to the output. [MGMT]